Editor's Note

BUSINESS SUCCESSION PLANNING

The tax brackets on the bottom of page 78 are 1998 brackets. The inflation adjusted brackets for year 2000 are as follows (corporate rates are not adjusted but are shown for comparison purposes):

Year 2000

Joint Individual Tax Rates		*Corporate Tax Rates* *	
Bracket	Rate	Bracket	Rate
$0 - $43,849	15%	$0 - $50,000	15%
$43,850 - $105,949	28%	$50,001 - $75,000	25%
$105,950 - $161,449	31%	$75,001 - $100,000	34%
$161,450 - $288,349	36%	$100,001 - $335,000	39%
$288,350 and over	39.6%	$335,001 - $10,000,000	34%
		$10,000,000 - $15,000,000	35%
		$15,000,001 - $18,333,332	38%
		$18,333,333 and over	35%

* Personal service corporations are taxed at a flat rate of 35%.

BUSINESS SUCCESSION PLANNING

DEARBORN™
A **Kaplan Professional** Company

This publication is designed to provide accurate and authoritative information in regard to the subject matter covered. It is sold with the understanding that the publisher is not engaged in rendering legal, accounting or other professional service. If legal advice or other expert assistance is required, the services of a competent professional person should be sought.

This text is updated periodically to reflect changes in laws and regulations. To verify that you have the most recent update, you may call Dearborn at 1-800-423-4723.

©2000 by Dearborn Financial Publishing, Inc.®
Published by Dearborn Financial Institute, Inc.®

Printed in the United States of America.

First printing, March 2000

Library of Congress Cataloging-in-Publication Data

Winn, Paul, 1940-
    Business succession planning / Paul J. Winn.
        p. cm.
    ISBN 0-7931-3951-1 (paper)
    1. Family-owned business enterprises--United States--Succession. 2. Family-owned business enterprises--Law and legislation--United States. 3. Business enterprises--Registration and transfer--United States. 4. Estate planning--United States.
I. Title

KF1382 .W56 2000
346.7305'2--dc21

                                            00-025631

····· Table of Contents

▪▪▪▪▪ Introduction

T he ability to add value to the life insurance sale is what sets one life insurance practitioner apart from another. That ability comes, in part, from a deep understanding of the problems and concerns of the client. In *Business Succession Planning*, the reader is brought face to face with those concerns as the book examines the practical issues that the business owner addresses in deciding how to dispose of a family business interest at death, disability or retirement. *Business Succession Planning* can help even the most expert life insurance practitioner stay attuned to this important market.

We wish to acknowledge Paul J. Winn, CLU, ChFC, who wrote this text. A published author, he is a former agent, agency head and home office executive who currently writes and edits training programs for financial services professionals.

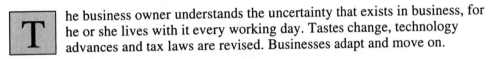

1

Why Plan for Business Succession?

T he business owner understands the uncertainty that exists in business, for he or she lives with it every working day. Tastes change, technology advances and tax laws are revised. Businesses adapt and move on.

Change, however, is not limited to markets, technology and the bottom line. It is a part of everything around us, including life itself. Life is fundamentally uncertain. In the space of a moment, it can change dramatically and irrevocably. It is to that kind of change, as well, that business must adapt. It is business' adapting to significant change—death, disability and retirement of an owner—that this book is about.

Life insurance agents and other financial services practitioners play an important role in ensuring that businesses and their owners are able to adapt to the loss of an owner by making certain they know how to apply their products. Life insurance can be used to help replace the value of the lost owner to the organization and plays a major role in facilitating the change of ownership.

Chapter Objectives

In this chapter, you will learn:

- what events bring about the need for ownership succession;

- the obstacles and impediments faced by businesses in their attempt to continue operating despite the loss of an owner;

- the costs that a business faces upon the loss of a key person;

- the options available to businesses when an owner dies;

- the need to establish the value of the business; and

- the steps that must be taken to implement a business succession plan.

■ ■ ■ ■ ■

■ WHEN BUSINESS SUCCESSION IS NEEDED

A business often owes its success to the drive, vision and creative energy of its owner or owners. When an owner leaves the business, regardless of the reason, it has an impact—sometimes an enormous one. Although the job of replacing a creative and visionary owner entirely may be impossible, it is possible to ease that loss through advance planning. This is the primary function of planning for business succession from the perspective of the business and its remaining owners.

The perspective of the surviving family, however, is somewhat different. The survivors often need to replace the family income that the business provided. Accomplishing that may entail continuing to operate the business or extracting the value of the owner's interest as quickly and with as little value loss as possible. As you can see, effective business succession planning must encompass the needs of the business, the needs of any remaining owners and the needs of the heirs.

Business succession is needed primarily to deal with three events that can result in the loss of a business owner. Those three events are:

1. the death of an owner;

2. the disability of an owner; and

3. the retirement of an owner.

Although the date of an owner's retirement is often known well in advance, death or disability may come at any time and may be entirely without warning.

Planning for business succession involves grappling with certain fundamental issues that affect the business. For example, the business owner must consider how his or her interest should be disposed of in the event of death, disability or retirement. Should the business be continued, or is liquidation a desirable option? If the business should be continued, should it be retained in the family?

Is a family member already a part of the business? If not, is there a family member interested in and capable of running it?

If there are no family members as potential successors, should the business be sold? Are there other partners or co-stockholders in the business to whom it should be sold? Is there an employee interested in owning the business some day? Is there a competitor that might be a possible purchaser of the business?

When some of these basic but vital decisions have been made by the business owner with the assistance of his or her advisors, a draft agreement that sets out the terms of the succession plan is produced. The necessary insurance products are purchased and referenced in the document, known as the buy-sell agreement, and the agreement is finalized and signed. Getting from the initial decisions, however, to a completed and funded buy-sell agreement that sets out the plan for business succession requires a myriad of interim considerations and decisions that we will explore together in the pages to come.

■ LEGAL IMPEDIMENTS TO CONTINUATION

One of the basic decisions that needs to be made by the business owner is whether the business should be continued or liquidated. That is not to suggest that any business can be effectively continued—or should be. Nothing could be further from the truth—at least not without some important planning.

By the end of 1990, there were approximately 3.8 million corporations in the United States, a number which attests to the popularity of incorporation. However, at the same time, there were 1.5 million active partnerships and 14.8 million sole proprietorships. A quick calculation tells us that 81 percent of businesses are unincorporated. Let's consider what that means with respect to the possible continuation of these unincorporated businesses at an owner's death.

The Sole Proprietor's Dilemma

Unlike corporations, which have continuous life, sole proprietorships and partnerships end upon the death of the sole proprietor or partner unless there is a plan, evidenced by a writing that states otherwise. If a sole proprietor dies, all of the owner's assets—including business assets—are subject to estate administration.

Unless there are clear instructions otherwise given in the will, the deceased sole proprietor's personal representative must accumulate the estate assets, including business assets, and convert them into cash. That cash is then used to pay any remaining debts of the owner, taxes (including estate taxes) and estate administration costs. Federal estate taxes, which may reduce the assets by as much as 55 percent in the larger estate, must generally be paid within nine months of the sole proprietor's death. Anything that is left is distributed according to the will.

Although the personal representative will, typically, attempt to sell the sole proprietorship as a going concern, the likelihood of effecting such a sale within the time available without prior planning is small. The reality is that it is so unlikely that it should not even be considered a possibility. Furthermore, if the personal representative continues to operate the business while attempting to find a buyer for the sole proprietorship, he or she may be taking on an unintended liability.

If the business continues to operate, like businesses generally, it will either produce a profit or a loss. If the continued operation results in a profit, that profit will go to the estate; the personal representative cannot benefit from it, even if the profit is entirely the result of his or her efforts. Losses, however, are treated much differently. If the continued operation of the business by the personal representative results in a loss, he or she is personally liable for it. So, for the personal representative, continuing the business can only result in loss—never a gain.

Because of the nature of the sole proprietorship, much of the owner's excess earnings over the years may have been reinvested in the business—often taking the form of inventory. As a result, the typical sole proprietorship is ordinarily non-liquid.*

---

* Liquidity is generally defined as the ability to convert an investment—in this case, a business—into cash quickly and with little or no loss in value.

Because the business may be non-liquid, the personal representative may be forced to sell the business for much less than its value as a going concern to pay the estate settlement costs, including estate taxes. In a forced sale, the cash received may be far less than half of the business' value as an operating business. For the sole proprietor and his or her family, business succession and succession planning should be seen as inextricably joined. They can't have the former without the latter.

Partnerships Die with the Death of a Partner

An effective general partnership results from a unique intermarriage of the talents and abilities of the individual partners. When a partnership works especially well,

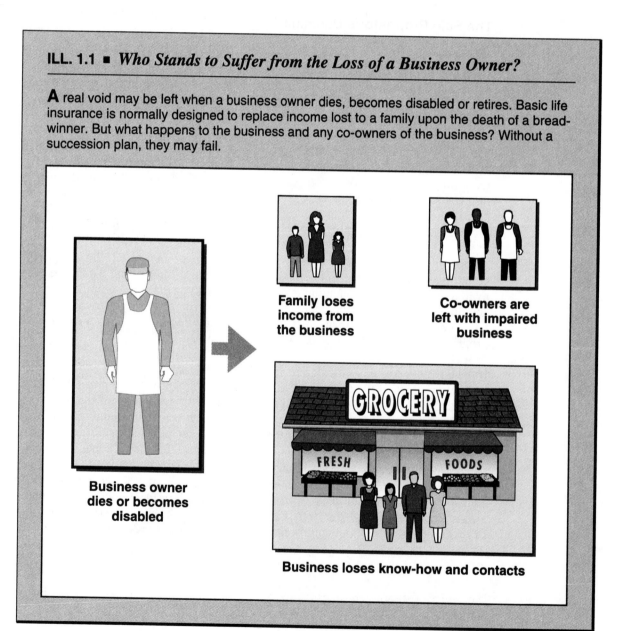

ILL. 1.1 ■ *Who Stands to Suffer from the Loss of a Business Owner?*

A real void may be left when a business owner dies, becomes disabled or retires. Basic life insurance is normally designed to replace income lost to a family upon the death of a breadwinner. But what happens to the business and any co-owners of the business? Without a succession plan, they may fail.

Business owner dies or becomes disabled

Family loses income from the business

Co-owners are left with impaired business

GROCERY

FRESH   FOODS

Business loses know-how and contacts

the coming together of individuals produces a result greater than the total of their particular talents. It is this synergism that often causes individuals to form the partnership in the first place.

The laws affecting partners and general partnerships reinforce this close interrelatedness of partners. The concept is called joint and several liability. What it means for the partners and the partnership is that:

- each partner is personally liable for the expenses and debts of the partnership; and

- each act of the partner—whether contractual or negligent—is attributable to each of the other partners.

Furthermore, the partners' liability is not limited to their financial contributions to the partnership. Instead, the liability extends also to the personal assets of the partners, including their savings, automobiles and homes.

If it seems that effective partnerships require a large share of mutual trust in addition to complementary partner skills, you're right. This is the fundamental philosophy underlying why, in the absence of a written agreement to the contrary, partnerships die with the death of a partner.

When a partner dies, the special combination of talents in the partnership no longer exists. If the surviving partners were required to accept a deceased partner's heir into the partnership in his or her stead, the mutual trust that is required between the surviving partners and the heir would not exist either. So, upon the death of a partner, the partnership ends. For the deceased partner's heirs, that may mean the end of their income. For the surviving partners, their partner's death may mean the end of their livelihood as well.

■ LOSING A KEY PERSON

Few things can be as devastating to a business as losing its key people. The obvious result to the organization of the loss of a key person is the loss of his or her services. A less obvious result of the loss of a key person may be the cost to recruit and train a replacement. In addition, a business' credit may hinge on the assurance that the loss of a key individual will not affect the organization's profitability.

Key People Provide Vital Services to the Business

The key person may be responsible for any aspect of the business' operation, such as sales, production or maintaining good relationships with the firm's customers. In addition, the individual's being a part of the organization may have had a positive impact on its available credit. In light of the foregoing, it's not unreasonable to define a key person as someone whose death would have an adverse economic effect on the business, caused by a loss of profits or credit standing and the expense of locating and hiring a capable replacement.

The decision to form a business is often the result of a realization that a greater business result can be achieved if individual resources—financial, managerial and other—can be combined. The death or disability of any key people may destroy this combination. The reason for the loss of profit at the death or disability of any one of the individuals will depend, of course, on the attributes and skills that the person brought to the business. Where those particular skills are management and leadership skills, not only the efficiency but also the direction of the firm may suffer.

Business Credit—The Lifeline to Profits

Business, especially small business, often relies heavily on credit. This might be credit available from the business' banking connection or credit advanced by suppliers. Whatever the source of credit, it is a lifeline for the typical business organization. With available credit, the business may flourish; without it, many businesses wither and die.

The credit that these sources are willing to extend may be adversely affected by the loss of a key person. Suppliers, even those that have done business with the firm for years, may be less likely to extend liberal credit terms to a business in which the potential sudden loss of a key person could disrupt its profitable operation. Upon the death or disability of such a key person, the business could expect its available credit to tighten even more.

Banking relationships are enormously important to many firms. Just like suppliers, banks may hold the key to the firm's existence as well as its growth. A bank that is considering a loan to a business normally looks at and assesses the firm's various strengths and weaknesses. Among those things that a bank usually examines are the firm's:

- cash position;

- management depth and ability;

- credit standing; and

- potential to produce profit.

When a business fails to meet the bank's standards in these areas, it may decline to extend credit. If it does extend credit, it may offer it only at a relatively high interest rate. In either case, the position of the business and its future profits are compromised.

Replacing the Key Person

When considering the effect on the business of the loss of a key person, it's important to keep in mind that, if the individual is truly a key person, his or her skills and talents must be replaced. Replacing these lost talents doesn't mean that the firm must find an additional clerical employee or even a middle manager, either of which may be in relatively large supply in the existing labor pool. In many cases, the firm will need to find a senior executive. Finding that senior executive may be both difficult and costly.

Consider the steps that must be taken to replace a key person. The business must locate that individual, attract him or her and, finally, train the new executive—and it must do that when its own profits, cash flow and, possibly, its future may be in jeopardy. Locating the individual can be delegated to an executive recruitment firm. Although the search for an acceptable replacement may take some time, it is not only time that is at stake; recruitment fees can amount to one-half of the executive's first year compensation or more.

Attracting the right person may also provide a real challenge for the business. Hiring a capable replacement may require that the business pay greater compensation than the amount that had been paid to the departed key person, especially if the key person had been an owner. As an owner, the key person could expect to receive income based solely on his or her ownership stake, an income source not usually available to the replacement. Salary is not the only motivation that the replacement might have; special executive benefits and the payment of relocation costs may be necessary.

Finally, once the right individual has been located and hired, he or she must be trained in the specific areas needed and in the firm's particular culture and procedures. It may be a year or more before the replacement executive can fully assume the responsibilities of the lost key person and become another key person. During that period the business will have expended large sums of money to replace the key person and may have lost substantial profits as the new executive settles in to the position.

As long ago as 1951, a United States Court of Appeals recognized the value of a business' key people and the legitimate business purpose in insuring them. In its opinion in a key case* the Court of Appeals declared:

> *What corporate purpose could be considered more essential than keyman insurance? The business that insures its building and machinery and automobiles from every possible hazard can hardly be expected to exercise less care in protecting itself against the loss of two of its most vital assets—managerial skill and experience.*

The court's language suggests that not only does key person insurance serve a legitimate business purpose in a legal sense, it is also a sound business practice.

■ REORGANIZING FOR THE FUTURE

Often, the family business is more than just the breadwinner's employer. It is the locus about which many of the decisions in the family revolve. For many business people, the family business represents not only the source of the lion's share of the family's income but also the principal creative outlet for the business owner. Upon the death or disability of that business owner, both the family and the business need to reorganize for the future. The plans they made before that time may have an enormous impact on the family's continued income and the viability of the business.

---

* *The Emeloid Co., Inc. v. Commissioner*, 189 Fed. 2d 230, (1951).

The two most desirable approaches to dealing with the death of a business owner and reorganizing for the future are:

1. retaining the business in the family; or

2. selling the business as a going concern.

Family Retention of the Business

Not all businesses should be retained by the family upon the death of the business owner any more than every person should be an entrepreneur. There must be a "fit" among the demands of the business, the requirements of the surviving family and the abilities of potential successors. In the first place, businesses that may be suitable for family retention are generally organized either as sole proprietorships or as corporations. Partnerships require the consent of the surviving partners for the heirs to assume the deceased business owner's role in the business, irrespective of the wishes of the deceased business owner's family.

There are a number of factors that favor family retention of a business besides its form of organization, however. Principal among those factors are:

- the availability of successor management;

- the profitability of the business;

- the salability of the business; and

- a tradition of family ownership.

Availability of Successor Management

Employee-Heirs.   It seems unnecessary to say it, but it bears repeating. Nobody usually cares more about a business and its success than its owner. What that means for the retention of the family business is that the most desirable manager of the family business that is to be retained is usually an owner.

The spouse or child who has played an important role in the family business may be the most appropriate owner of the business when the former business owner dies. In addition to the desirability of carrying on the tradition of family ownership (we'll examine that shortly), elevating an existing employee who is also an heir to the senior management position offers other important benefits.

The heir who works in the business may already understand how the business operates. He or she will probably be familiar with the existing business culture and may understand the needs of the key accounts and requirements of the firm's suppliers.

Often, the heir will even know the people involved. The suppliers and customers that are acquainted and comfortable with the successor are considerably more likely to continue to extend credit to and purchase from the firm.

Arranging for an employee-heir to take the reins also avoids certain problems that other choices don't avoid—specifically, employee morale problems. Other employees expect that an heir working in the business may take over when the boss dies. Meeting that expectation can be important. He or she is a known quantity to the other employees. As a result, succession by an employee-heir, instead of an unknown outsider, is usually accompanied by far less employee anxiety and apprehension. Employees may be more likely to concentrate on doing their jobs rather than on the future of the company and the security of their income.

Sometimes a business owner and his or her family will want to retain the business upon the owner's death even though there are no heirs that have worked in the business, are capable of running it or have any interest in doing so. Although, for the reasons that have just been examined, an heir-employee may be the best choice as the successor manager, that may not be possible. The business owner may want to consider a current employee or an outsider.

Another Employee. A current employee who has been or will be exposed to the critical issues in running the company may be the next best choice as a successor to the business owner, provided he or she is interested in and capable of eventually managing the enterprise. Although this individual may not be an owner, either immediately or at any time in the future, a performance-based compensation arrangement may help to supply the financial motivation to act like one.

Not unlike some of the reasons that favor the employee-heir as successor, the current employee is known to the other employees. The successor's being known to the other employees will tend to settle their qualms about an unknown manager taking over and "cleaning house." Accordingly, morale is likely to be more positive with the elevation of an existing employee than with the installation of an outsider.

In addition, the current employee who has been identified as the successor will usually understand the firm's culture and probably be familiar with and to the company's suppliers and major customers. Because the existing employee is familiar with suppliers and customers, their comfort level with the new manager may be greater than it would be with an unknown replacement. For that reason, the business may encounter fewer problems in maintaining its credit lines and major customers.

An Outsider. Sometimes, there are just no suitable candidates on the inside to take over the management of the operation at the death of the business owner. It may still be possible for the family to retain the business by bringing in an outsider to run it.

Although an outsider may have fundamental management problems not encountered by the heir-successor or even by a current employee groomed to take over the reins, the appointment of an outsider may have almost as many positive aspects as negative ones. Let's examine both the positives and negatives. Before we do, however, we need to understand the minimum requirements of the successful outsider.

The successful outsider candidate chosen by the family to run the business needs to have certain background, abilities and skills that will enable him or her to more effectively manage. One of the most important of those is leadership ability.

Consider what has happened in the business from the perspective of the business, itself:

- The person most informed about the business is no longer available to help guide it.

- The vision that inspired the business and its employees is gone.

- The employees' trust in the company's management may have evaporated, and people may be concerned about their jobs and the future of the company.

Unlike the authority that comes with management and which is conferred from above, the role of "leader" is, of course, granted by those being led. For that reason, becoming the leader is a status that the outsider must earn. To be able to do that, the outsider must have and be able to communicate to his or her intended followers:

- vision

- credibility

- competence

In addition to being able to lead the company and its employees, the outsider must also possess management ability. He or she must be able to make the hard choices and go on. Often, those choices concern personnel issues that the business owner may have been unwilling to confront.

Business owners, especially those who began the business, may have employees who have remained with the company through both the good times and bad. While some of these employees may have been instrumental in the company's success, others may have been kept on the payroll simply because they exhibited a loyalty to the company and its owner while making little positive contribution to the success of the business. The new manager must be able to deal with unproductive employees in a businesslike manner, discharging those who fail to contribute.

Although sometimes of less consequence than the new manager's leadership and management ability, the most desirable outsider will usually possess industry knowledge. He or she should be familiar with the industry's culture, its processes and its key issues. Often, the outsider who is chosen to take over the management of the business is a senior executive in a competing firm. That executive may be acquainted with the principal suppliers and many of the major customers. More importantly, the suppliers may be comfortable with the new manager and be willing to continue their credit and delivery arrangements without interruption.

But what are the considerations that militate for and against the outsider—even one with outstanding management and leadership skills—as an appropriate replacement for the business owner? The most important negatives that may be encountered in appointing an outsider are:

- The outsider may be an unknown to the company's employees, leading to further erosion of employee morale.

- The outsider may be an unknown to the company's suppliers and bankers, resulting in a tightening of credit terms.

- The outsider may be unfamiliar with the firm's major customers, causing management missteps that lose customers.

- The outsider may not understand the industry, resulting in a loss of important company contacts.

Many of the negatives that militate against choosing an outsider to lead the company can be overcome by appointing a current high-level employee to act as the new manager's assistant. He or she can act as a buffer and "translator" between the new manager and the company's employees, suppliers and customers during the adjustment period until the successor can interact effectively with these constituents.

Bringing in an outsider to run the company, however, is not necessarily the worst idea. The change from business-owner management to professional management may lead to important business growth. Understanding how that could result requires an appreciation of the typical business owner's management style.

The typical small business owner is 10 percent entrepreneur, 20 percent manager and 70 percent technician.* As a result, the business owner often brings a technician's "doer" attitude to the enterprise, with its singular, parochial focus. The infusion of professional management and its generally broader perspective may make a substantial difference in the future of the firm.

The professional manager is, by definition, not a technician. He or she will often lack the technical expertise of the business owner. As a result, the manager must achieve results through others. In a word, the manager must manage. Because the technical work is not being done by the manager, he or she has a greater opportunity to view the business *as a business*. With this broader perspective, the manager may just bring the business to heights that would have been impossible for the owner.

Company Profitability

Consider the great loss that would have occurred if Bill Gates had died or become disabled before Microsoft had come into its own and the family had decided, as a result, to liquidate the business. Microsoft had enormous future profitability that would have evaporated. The same thinking needs to go into the decision to retain or dispose of any family business.

When the business is in an industry experiencing a high rate of growth, such as the computer industry experienced in its early years, family retention may make considerably more sense than liquidation or sale. Similarly, when the business holds assets whose value can be expected to inflate—such as real property—the growth potential of the business assets must be carefully considered. If respected observers anticipate continued growth in the industry or for particular business assets, family retention should be strongly considered.

---

* Michael E. Gerber, *The E Myth* (Cambridge: Ballinger, 1986), p. 20.

Business Salability

Some businesses are inherently less liquid than other businesses. This, too, should play a part in the family's decision to hold onto or dispose of the business.

A business in a forced sale situation may bring a price that is one-half or less than its value as an ongoing business. Particularly if the forced disposition of the business results in great financial loss to the surviving family, the business owner may want to ensure that appropriate provisions are made for its retention.

A Tradition of Family Ownership

Some businesses have become almost inextricably identified with a particular family. That identification may help to ensure customer loyalty as well as favorable supplier terms and bank credit. When a business and a family have developed so close an identification in the mind of those outside the business, its retention by the family may be even more appropriate. That fact, of course, does not diminish the importance of the availability of successor management or the likelihood of long-term business profitability. It is, however, another decisional factor for the business owner to keep in mind in planning for business succession.

Adequate Estate Liquidity

None of the considerations that we have examined—successor management availability, favorable long-term business prospects or a family ownership tradition—matter at all if the business must be sold to meet estate settlement costs. If the business owner's estate has insufficient cash to pay estate taxes and other estate settlement costs, a forced sale of the business may be necessary despite the business owner's and his or her family's intention to retain it.

We will examine the important estate planning issues in Chapter 3 when we look more closely at the concerns that must be faced by the family seeking to retain a business. Provided the business owner is insurable, however, the appropriate solution to the problem of limited estate liquidity usually involves the purchase of a suitable amount of life insurance on the business owner's life.

Selling the Business as a Going Concern

Not all family businesses should be retained in the family. It may be more appropriate to sell the family business at the death or disability of the business owner. The question, of course, is: "To whom might the business be sold?" There may be several answers to this question for any particular business.

Selling to Other Owners

The most obvious choice of a suitable buyer for the business is another owner, if there is one. Although this approach to disposing of the business would not be appropriate for the sole proprietorship since, by definition, it has no other owners, it may be the most desirable alternative for the partnership or the corporation having co-shareholders.

The Partners as Purchasers.   Since a partnership is a voluntary relationship, the right to choose one's partner is a fundamental principle. Therefore, when a partner dies, the partnership, by law, dissolves. Without an agreement to the contrary, the surviving partner becomes a liquidating trustee. His or her job is to wrap up the affairs of the partnership.

As a liquidating trustee, the surviving partner may not continue to operate the business without the consent of the former partner's heirs. To do so would subject the partner to complete liability for losses but no participation in profits.

Instead, the liquidating trustee must:

- complete any partnership obligations that were begun prior to the former partner's death;

- collect any accounts receivable;

- pay any accounts payable;

- convert any partnership assets to cash; and

- distribute any remaining cash to the deceased partner's estate and any other partners according to their interest

— or —

- assess the deceased partner's estate and any other partners for any debts remaining after liquidation of the partnership assets.

In short, the surviving partner—as liquidating trustee—must put himself or herself out of business.

For the surviving partner, the prospect is a particularly dim one. The partner stands to lose his or her livelihood and, possibly, suffer a substantial asset loss. Without an agreement to the contrary, his or her choices are two: to reach an agreement with new partners to establish a new company or liquidate and distribute partnership assets. Neither choice may be particular appealing. A happier choice for both the surviving partner and the deceased partner's family may be for the surviving partners to purchase the deceased partner's interest from his or her estate. Such an arrangement may solve the surviving family's and the surviving partner's problems. Let's consider what each, typically, needs.

For the surviving partner or partners, the most fundamental business need may be to continue the business as it existed before the death of their partner. If the surviving partners continue the business, their income and livelihood will continue. Furthermore, their assets that are tied up in the business will not be depleted by a forced sale.

For the deceased partner's family, selling the business at the best price may also be the most appropriate choice. Their principal immediate financial concerns are usually for a resumption of income and an inflow of cash to meet death-related expenses. Selling the business may satisfy both concerns.

In many families, the business may have provided the family livelihood and little more. The death of the business owner has meant the loss of that income. So, the first consideration is its replacement. Since income is generated either by people at work or money at work, capital must replace the deceased partner's earning power. That capital can come from the purchase price paid by the surviving partners for the business.

In addition to providing replacement income for the surviving family members, the purchase price of the business paid by the partners can help to meet the deceased partner's estate's liquidity needs. Since the bulk of the estate of many business owners is composed of non-liquid assets, many estates experience a serious lack of cash to pay estate settlement costs.

Whether the partner's loss to the partnership is due to his or her death, disability or retirement, the need may be the same for both the family and the surviving partners. That need is to extract the value of the departed or departing partner's share of the business while enabling the business to continue operating as a going concern. There needs to be a transfer of capital from the business to the family *without depleting the business' capital*. The only way to do that is through cash that is generated by the event that produces the need for the cash—life and disability insurance.

Co-Stockholders as Purchasers. Unlike the partnership form of business, corporations have continual life. They don't end at the death of a stockholder. To the extent that corporations continue beyond the life span of their owners, the problem of business dissolution faced by the surviving partners is avoided by the co-stockholders. A separate problem, however, takes its place.

Absent some form of restriction on the alienation of stock shares, shares of stock are freely transferable. They may be sold or assigned as collateral during the stockholder's life. At the stockholder's death, they generally pass through the deceased stockholder's will just as any other form of property that he or she owned at death. For the surviving stockholders, that free transferability may be almost as disastrous as partnership dissolution.

Since stock shares are generally transferable, the heirs stand in the ownership position of the deceased stockholder. If the heirs were a part of the business and being groomed for succession during the stockholder's life, their ownership may not be particularly problematic. However, when an inexperienced—and, possibly, youthful—heir uses the inheritance to vote himself or herself into a position of authority in the firm, the resulting damage may be incalculable.

The direction of the business may change. The strategic plans that were designed and implemented may be scrapped. Dividends, seldom declared in the close corporation, may be authorized. Although it is impossible to determine beforehand just how any business will be affected by the presence of new and inexperienced owners, that it *will* be affected is almost certain.

Despite the possibly disastrous effects on a business of the entry of new owners, the problems are usually caused not by any malice but by a difference in objectives between the new owners and the surviving stockholders. The surviving stockholders may want to continue business as usual while the deceased stockholder's heirs who are the new stockholders may want immediate cash. Although the problem of inexperienced heirs may be greater in those cases in which the deceased stockholder held a majority interest, minority stockholder interests can also disrupt the effective running of a company.

The answer for both the surviving heirs and the surviving co-stockholders is the same as it is in the partnership form of organization. In many cases, the deceased stockholder's ownership interest in the business should be sold to the surviving stockholders who can maintain the business as a going concern.

Selling to Employees

In the event that it is inadvisable to retain a family business and there are no partners or co-stockholders to purchase the deceased business owner's interest, it may be appropriate to consider selling the interest to an employee. The employee may be a sales person familiar with the business' major customers, an inside manager who runs the company's internal operations or any other valuable employee.

The sale to an employee would guarantee the value of the business to the surviving heirs and would ensure, for the employees, that the business would continue following the death, disability or retirement of the business owner. In addition, selecting an outstanding employee to purchase the business would help to retain the employee and keep him or her motivated. An important issue in the sale of the business is always obtaining the necessary funds to effect it. For many employees, that is a major obstacle. That important subject will be treated, in depth, in Chapter 4.

Selling to a Competitor

Although selling the business as a going concern to other owners or to an employee may be the easiest to arrange, they are not the only possibilities. In the event that neither of these possibilities is appropriate, a sale of the business to a competitor may be indicated.

While business sales to a competitor at the death of the business owner are generally the most difficult to arrange, the actual process is strikingly similar to any other buyout arrangement. The principal obstacle lies in finding the right competitor. From the heirs' point of view, the result is identical to any other business sale. The business is sold, and the heirs receive cash for their share of it.

■ LOCKING IN BUSINESS VALUES

A business ordinarily has a market value that is far in excess of the sum of its assets. In fact, the most important factor in determining the value of a particular business is not the extent of its assets at all, which may play an exceedingly small role in calculating value. Instead, the most important factor is its earnings capacity. However, when a business is liquidated, that earnings capacity plays no part in determining what is received for it. The value represented by the earnings capacity is lost forever. A vitally important benefit of planning for business succession is the ability to establish a price for the business that locks in its value as an operating business rather than as a liquidated one.

Valuing the Business

Determining the value of a public corporation—a corporation listed on a stock exchange—is a relatively easy matter. Its value can be calculated by multiplying the price for a share of its stock by the number of shares outstanding. For businesses that are not public corporations—and that includes most of the businesses in the United States—determining value is considerably more difficult.

In planning for business succession, valuing the business and establishing that value in the document that provides for the sale provides a number of benefits.

Accordingly, the well-drawn document—known as the buy-sell agreement—contains an important valuation clause. The buy-sell valuation clause:

- eliminates the need to haggle over the value of the business;

- helps the parties to the agreement plan for retirement and estate transfer; and

- may set the value of the business for estate tax purposes.

Generally, there are four ways to fix a value for a business. These are:

1. book value

2. agreed value

3. appraisal value

4. formula valuation

Each of these approaches to establishing a value for a business has its benefits and drawbacks. An extensive analysis and discussion of business valuation will be provided in Chapter 6.

Providing Liquidity

Whether the business is to be retained by the family or sold to others, an infusion of cash into the transaction is needed. A determination of the value of and the price to be paid for a business is, of course, very important. However, without also ensuring that the buyers have ample liquidity to carry out the sale, valuation becomes little more than an interesting but pointless exercise.

The same is true of the business succession plan that envisions retention of the business by the family. Unless appropriate provisions are made for guaranteeing that there is sufficient liquidity to cushion the business during the transitional period as well as enough cash in the estate to satisfy any estate settlement liabilities, plans for retaining the business may fail. Failure may be the result of insufficient business cash flow to meet ongoing business needs or may be caused by the need to sell the business to raise money to pay estate taxes.

Whether the plan calls for retention or sale, there are three methods of providing the funds needed to meet liquidity needs. They are:

1. cash from current operating revenue;

2. borrowed funds; and

3. life insurance.

What is the cost to the business of using each of these three ways of providing liquidity to purchase the deceased business owner's interest at his or her death? We will assume, for simplicity, that the business is incorporated and is taxed as a regular corporation. In the approaches we will examine, the assumptions are as follows:

1. The business is valued at $5,000,000.

2. The cost to borrow funds is 10 percent.

3. The deceased business owner is 45 years old.

4. The deceased business owner's shares will be redeemed by the business.

5. The business is in a 34 percent income tax bracket.

Because redeeming shares of the deceased business owner is not tax deductible, a business in a 34 percent income tax bracket must earn $1.52 to have $1.00 to spend. Of the $1.52 that is earned by the business, $.52 is paid in taxes. When this arithmetic is applied to a $5,000,000 business purchase, the result is eye opening.

Buying the Business Interest for Cash

Let's use this arithmetic to determine the cost to the corporation of a cash redemption of the business owner's shares. To simplify matters, we will assume that the shares will be purchased over a five-year period, and no interest will be charged.

To have $1,000,000 to cover the five annual payments, the corporation must earn $1,515,152. After five years, the corporation would have paid the $5,000,000 needed to fund the buyout of the deceased business owner's shares *and an additional $2,575,760 in income tax*. The business' decision to buy out the shareholder's interest using current operating revenues increased its liability almost 52 percent!

Year	Cash Payment	Pre-Tax Earnings Required
1	$1,000,000	$1,515,152
2	$1,000,000	$1,515,152
3	$1,000,000	$1,515,152
4	$1,000,000	$1,515,152
5	$1,000,000	$1,515,152
	$5,000,000	$7,575,760

In the real world, of course, deferred payments over a five-year period would, almost certainly, include interest. Although that interest may be a business expense that is deductible to the corporation as interest incurred in the conduct of a trade or business, it would, nonetheless, add to the cost to redeem the shares. Let's consider the impact of interest when we look at the result on the corporation if it uses borrowed funds to complete the buyout.

Buying the Business Interest Using Borrowed Funds

In this illustration we will assume that the business has negotiated a loan from its lending source to fund the purchase of the deceased stockholder's shares. Since the loan repayment could represent a significant cash flow drain, lenders may be reluctant to extend the necessary credit. If the credit is extended for purposes of making the buyout, it may affect the company's available credit for other purposes, such as inventory. The only light at the end of this tunnel is that the annual interest the corporation will pay is fully tax deductible.

In addition to tying up the firm's valuable credit line, using borrowed funds to complete the buyout of the shareholder's interest actually will cost the company an additional $4,075,760 in interest on the loan and income taxes on funds needed to repay the loan principal. That increases the cost to effect the buyout by 81.5 percent.

Here is a year-by-year illustration of the total cost of the buyout and how the business cash flow would be affected.

Year	Year-End Principal Repayment	Remaining Loan Balance	Interest Payment on Balance	Pre-Tax Earnings Required
1	$1,000,000	$5,000,000	$500,000	$2,015,152
2	$1,000,000	$4,000,000	$400,000	$1,915,152
3	$1,000,000	$3,000,000	$300,000	$1,815,152
4	$1,000,000	$2,000,000	$200,000	$1,715,152
5	$1,000,000	$1,000,000	$100,000	$1,615,152
	$5,000,000		$1,500,000	$9,075,760

Buying the Business Interest Using Life Insurance Proceeds

The final—and, as we will see shortly, preferable—method of redeeming the deceased shareholder's interest is through the use of life insurance proceeds. Although the premiums paid are not a deductible expense, the significantly larger death benefits are usually income tax free.

Year	Annual Premium*	Pre-Tax Earnings Required	Cumulative Pre-Tax Earnings Required	Death Benefit
1	$29,700	$45,000	$45,000	$5,000,000
2	$29,700	$45,000	$90,000	$5,000,000
10	$29,700	$45,000	$450,000	$5,000,000
11	$29,700	$45,000	$495,000	$5,000,000
15	$29,700	$45,000	$675,000	$5,000,000
16	$29,700	$45,000	$720,000	$5,000,000
20	$29,700	$45,000	$900,000	$5,000,000

* Based on representative male, age 45, non-smoker rates for permanent life insurance.

The time value of money, the timing of the stockholder's death and the likelihood that out-of-pocket premiums may not be required for the entire policy duration (because they may be offset by dividends or unnecessary due to excess interest) have not been taken into account. Although the illustrated numbers ignore these important issues for the purposes of simplicity, the difference in the cost of the various methods can, nonetheless, be appreciated. The difference is nothing short of startling.

Comparison of Cost of Buyout Funding Methods

Cash	Borrowed Funds	Life Insurance Proceeds*
$7,575,760	$9,075,760	$900,000

* For illustration purposes only; ignores the time value of money, timing of death and the possibility that premiums may not be required out-of-pocket for the entire duration of the policy.

■ SUMMARY

This chapter has presented the reasons why planning for business succession is critical in withstanding the departure—voluntary of involuntary—of the business owner and to the surviving family's ability to maintain its income. The legal impediments to continuation of the business that are faced by sole proprietorships and partnerships have been examined, as have the substantial costs that are incurred by businesses when they lose a key person. The chapter has also presented the options available when a business owner dies and the decisional factors that should be taken into account when considering family retention or sale of the business.

The reasons for valuing a business were discussed, and the customary methods for doing a valuation were introduced. Finally, the subject of liquidity was examined and various funding options for buying the deceased business owner's interest were discussed and compared.

■ CHAPTER 1 QUESTIONS FOR REVIEW

1. Under the law, what is the function of a surviving partner following his or her partner's death?

    A. To seek as much additional business as possible to financially assist the deceased partner's family

    B. To wrap up the business

    C. To immediately seek a replacement for the deceased partner

    D. To immediately enter into a partnership with the heirs of the deceased partner

2. Which of the following statements is NOT true concerning a general partnership?

    A. Each partner is personally liable for the expenses and debts of the partnership.

    B. Acts of the partner are attributable to each of the other partners.

    C. A general partner can avoid liability for debts of the partnership by agreement with the other partners.

    D. A partner's liability for partnership debts extends to the partner's personal assets.

3. Which of the following business organizations has perpetual life?

    A. Corporation

    B. General partnership

    C. Limited partnership

    D. Sole proprietorship

4. How soon after the death of a business owner must any federal estate taxes usually be paid?

    A. Six months

    B. Nine months

    C. Twelve months

    D. Two years

5. Generally, the least costly method of providing liquidity to a business to purchase a deceased owner's interest is

    A. borrowed funds

    B. installment payments of cash from the ongoing operations of the business

    C. a single payment of cash from the ongoing operations of the business

    D. life insurance proceeds

2
Alternatives to Succession

P assing the business along as a going concern—to heirs, partners, co-stockholders, employees or competitors—upon the death, disability or retirement of the business owner is unquestionably the option that usually makes the most sense for everyone involved. The heirs receive the greatest value, other owners can continue their livelihood uninterrupted, and valued employees can continue to earn a living without being professionally dislocated. Sometimes, however, business succession just isn't an option.

Liquidation of a business is usually the last alternative when nothing else—sale of the business or family retention—is a viable option. However, even if liquidation is the only avenue for the business, the business owner still has choices. The business owner can plan for liquidation of the business, or he or she can just "let it happen." The difference for the heirs can be dramatic.

Chapter Objectives

In this chapter, you will learn:

- what conditions or situations point to the advisability of liquidation;

- the adverse consequences of unplanned liquidation;

- the results of planned liquidation; and

- the steps that must be taken to liquidate a business while preserving as much of its value as possible.

■ ■ ■ ■ ■

■ LIQUIDATING THE BUSINESS WITHOUT A PLAN: THE WORST CASE

Time Is the Single Greatest Enemy

A well-known 17th century English poem urges the poet's mistress to be aware that time is short and is the enemy of their relationship. For the business that is to be liquidated by default—which is to say, without a plan—time continues to be the enemy.

Whether the business liquidator is the surviving partner or the estate's executor, the problem is fundamentally the same: Absent a plan, business assets must be converted to cash as quickly as possible. Without a plan evidenced by a writing, the sole proprietorship or partnership must be terminated. However, it is not only unincorporated businesses that face dissolution upon the departure of a business owner; close corporations often experience the same fate upon the death, disability or retirement of a majority shareholder.

While corporations theoretically enjoy perpetual life, the close corporation may be heavily dependent upon the departed majority shareholder's management skills, contacts or customer and supplier relationships. All businesses, regardless of their form of organization, face the problem of liquidation when their success is derived principally from the skills, talents and creative energy of a single individual. As a result, despite the perpetual life of the corporation, the loss of a major shareholder-officer may mean the end of the business.

A major factor in the liquidation of many businesses is the requirement that estate taxes be paid within nine months following the business owner's death. Since interests in closely held businesses are generally illiquid, coming up with sufficient cash upon the death of the owner to pay those taxes and other estate transfer costs can result in an unplanned liquidation. A few things that turn out better when they are spontaneous and unplanned may exist, but business liquidation is not one of them. Let's turn our attention, now, to the unfortunate consequences of an unplanned liquidation.

Consequences of Unplanned Liquidation

While the liquidation of a profitable business concern is seldom the most desirable option upon the death, disability or retirement of a business owner, it may be the *only* option in some cases. If liquidation is to be the course of action upon the departure of the business owner, the choice is either to plan for it or not. We will examine how to plan for it in the next section. First, let's look at what may happen if that important planning isn't done.

As we discussed just a short while ago, time is the unplanned liquidator's greatest enemy. Both the law and, often, the need for large amounts of cash quickly to pay estate transfer costs push the liquidator to make whatever arrangements are needed to convert the business into cash. What this means to the value of the business relates principally to the firm's accounts receivable and its other assets.

The unplanned liquidation often requires:

- the hurried collection of accounts receivable; and

- the forced sale of the business assets.

Because the accounts receivable must be collected quickly, they are often compromised at fifty cents or less on the dollar. Those accounts that cannot be collected directly from the debtors are generally sold to collection firms. Unfortunately, since many of these accounts will prove impossible to collect under any circumstances, the ARs may be sold for 5 or 10 percent of the actual amount owed the business being liquidated.

Although the compromising of many of the accounts receivable may be a significant loss for the business, the forced sale of the business assets may result in a much more substantial loss—both immediately and in the long term—to the surviving family members. When the business assets are sold in a forced sale, a number of consequences ensue.

- The remaining accounts receivable often bring just pennies on the dollar because they may be impossible to collect.

- Goodwill—the difference between the value of the firm as a going concern and its asset value—is lost completely. Because the business is being dismembered, there is no remaining goodwill to sell.

- The inventory, plan and fixtures are usually sold at fire-sale prices. Go to an estate sale sometime if you are looking for an outstanding value. Although the estate sale may result in an excellent deal for the buyer, the other side of the transaction does not fare nearly as well. The seller has given up much of the value of the assets in order to facilitate their sale.

- Because of the loss of goodwill and the value of the accounts receivable and fixed assets, the heirs have suffered a significant loss in the value of their assets.

- Representing, perhaps, the biggest loss of all, the surviving family members have lost their family income.

Liquidation of the assets of a business is seldom a happy prospect. When that liquidation is unplanned, the unhappy prospect may be compounded into financial tragedy. The answer to avoiding that financial tragedy when liquidation is the only viable option is to plan for an orderly liquidation.

■ THE PLANNED LIQUIDATION WHEN SUCCESSION ISN'T AN OPTION

Sometimes retention or sale of a business as an ongoing concern just isn't possible. In such a case, liquidation may be the only viable option. Knowing when liquidation is indicated may only be half the battle, but it's the important half. Let's examine those conditions that render the sale of a business or its retention by the family unworkable and, as a consequence, suggest liquidation.

Factors That Favor Business Liquidation

The factors that favor business liquidation, of course, are the opposite of those that suggest family retention or sale.

Heirs Uninterested or Incapable. The most appropriate successor owners of the business are the heirs that were a part of the business during the departed business owner's tenure and who are both interested in owning the business and capable of running it. When the heirs are uninterested in running the business or are not capable of taking it over, the business owner needs to acknowledge that serious impediment to family retention.

Successor Manager Unavailable. A professional manager from outside the company or an existing employee may be a workable substitute for the intimate, day-to-day involvement of an owner. Sometimes, the professional manager may even be a better choice to manage the organization than one of the heirs. The challenge for the business owner has to do with the availability of a successor manager and the cost to employ him or her, if available. Because the professional manager or existing employee may not be an owner either immediately or eventually, the business may need to pay the successor manager more income than was being taken by the departed business owner. If a successor manager for the business is either unavailable or unaffordable, family retention by heirs who are themselves uninterested or incapable of running the business should usually be ruled out.

Minimal Future Business Profitability. In a sense, businesses are like people. They are young at one time, they mature, get old and, eventually, they die. Their organization and profitability usually reflect where, in that continuum, they happen to be. Businesses, even those with a long history of profitable operations and talented management, may face a future of reduced profitability or even extinction. Consider the plight of the well-run buggy whip manufacturer at the advent of the automobile. Far more recently, manufacturers of typewriters have ceased operations or entered into other fields as computers with word processing programs have swept the market. If the family business has a history of marginally profitable or unprofitable operations—or if it faces an uncertain future because of the introduction of competing marketplace technology—the likelihood of selling it is small, and its retention by the family is inappropriate.

Non-Transferable Good Will. Some businesses, particularly personal service businesses, owe their success entirely to the indefinable qualities of the business owner. His or her way of doing business or relating to customers may be so unusual or effective as to be almost unique. When a particular attribute of the business owner that has been critical to business success can't be duplicated, the business may end when the owner departs, regardless of the form under which the business is organized. When that is the case, a strong argument can be made for liquidation.

Owner's Talent, Experience or Skill Can't Be Duplicated. Similar to non-transferable good will, there may be a certain unique combination of talents, experiences and skills possessed by an owner that have enabled him or her to create and manage a successful business. If those skills, talents and wealth of experience are not also possessed by the heirs—and can't be hired—the surviving family needs to assess how critical they are to maintaining the business. If they are deemed to be vital, family retention should not be considered. Additionally, if the unique qualities possessed by the business owner are seen to be the cause of the success of the business, selling the business as a going concern may not be possible. Liquidation may be the only choice left to the heirs.

Legal Impediments to Continuation. Some businesses are professional rather than commercial in nature. Think of the physician or dentist that you consult, or the attorney who drafted your will. He or she may be a sole proprietor, partner or stockholder. In general, anyone who must obtain a license from the state to practice is considered a professional. While it may be obvious that a non-professional cannot hold himself or herself out as a professional, it may be less obvious that the non-professional cannot be a partner in a professional partnership or stockholder in a professional corporation. If the professional practice cannot be sold and there are no heirs professionally qualified to step into it, liquidation is the only option.

Non-Transferable Employee Loyalty. Some people inspire personal loyalty from their employees far beyond what might normally be expected. If the business owner is such an individual, he or she needs to consider the result of that personal loyalty on a potential successor. Can the employees be expected to transfer that loyalty to the new owner? Will they leave when the new owner fails to inspire the same kind of loyalty? If that employee loyalty can't be transferred, there is less likelihood that a successor owner can operate the business successfully.

Business Continuation Entails Substantial Risk. The business owner normally accepts risk as the price of success. For the heirs, however, substantial risk may be a constant cause of concern and frustration. They may be much more concerned with financial *survival* rather than business success, and that risk may ultimately result in business failure. If running the business will involve substantial risk, liquidation may be a wiser choice than retaining the business in the family.

Lack of a Successor Owner. Although a successor owner may be a partner, co-stockholder, employee or an outsider, selling the business owner's interest may not be possible for any number of reasons. If no successor owner can be located and family retention of the business is not feasible, liquidation may be the appropriate answer.

Extracting Maximum Value from the Business

If retention of the business by the surviving family isn't an option and arranging for the sale of the business isn't possible, liquidation may be the only appropriate course of action. However, as we have already seen, an unplanned liquidation may result in the loss of more than half of the value that the business has as a going concern. Fortunately, an unplanned liquidation isn't the only choice. A far better choice is to plan for it. If the family is to avoid the enormous asset loss resulting from an unplanned liquidation and extract the maximum value from the business, the liquidation must be a planned liquidation. Let's examine what is required to turn the unplanned liquidation into an orderly planned liquidation.

Planning for liquidation has two facets. Those two facets are:

1. minimizing business value erosion; and

2. replacing the business value that has been eroded.

Minimizing Business Value Erosion

Minimizing the erosion of business value incident to the liquidation of the business requires that time be made available to the liquidator. That time is made available by a combination of testamentary provisions and life insurance.

Testamentary Provisions. Testamentary provisions are those that are made in the business owner's last will and testament. They should provide fairly broad powers to the liquidator—whether that is the business owner's executor or a former partner acting as a liquidating trustee—to act in a manner that is more likely to result in a greater price to be received for the business. In large measure, that means removing the "forced" from "forced sale." Let's examine how that can be accomplished.

Power to Sell. The will should give the executor, or the executor acting in concert with any surviving partners, the power to sell the business or the business owner's interest at the time and under the terms that are deemed most appropriate.

Power to Retain. The best time to sell aunt Mary's stock is not usually during a bear market. The same is true for a business or a business interest. Selling the business intact or in pieces may be more advantageous in six months than it is now.

The provisions of the will should give the executor or liquidating trustee the power to retain the business for as long as is deemed appropriate in order to ensure that the best price and terms can be arranged. By inserting such a clause in the will, the executor is assured that the compulsion to sell the business immediately has been lifted.

Power to Change Organizational Form. Sometimes, changing the organizational form of the business from a sole proprietorship or partnership to a corporation may facilitate the temporary retention of the business and expedite its sale as a going concern. For that reason, the executor or liquidating trustee should be given the power to change the form of business organization.

Hold Harmless. Giving the executor or liquidating trustee these fairly broad powers with respect to the business or business interest may result in minimizing the anticipated erosion that often results from liquidation. Unfortunately, they may not have this desired effect at all. In some cases, the executor's exercise of these powers may result in the family's receiving less, rather than more, for the business.

Incorporation of the partnership may not result in expediting the sale of the business at all, and the costs incident to the organizational change may have been substantial. The delay in selling the business until a more favorable climate is available may result in a lost opportunity, and the more favorable economic climate may never materialize. In a word, the executor, despite his or her best efforts, may be wrong.

To ensure that the executor or liquidating trustee takes those prudent risks that are designed to maximize the liquidation value of the business interest, he or she must be held harmless for the results of these actions. The final testamentary provision should free the executor or liquidating trustee from any personal liability that he or she reasonably takes with respect to the disposition of the business interest. The executor would, of course, continue to be liable for any unreasonable risks.

Life Insurance. The role of life insurance in prolonging the period of time that the executor or liquidating trustee has in disposing of the business interest is enormous. Let's examine this important element in the planning strategy.

Paying Estate Settlement Costs. One of the serious motivators in selling the business interest quickly is the need to pay estate settlement costs. These costs may include federal estate taxes, state death taxes and the various probate costs. In addition, the business may have outstanding debts that must be paid. By purchasing life insurance in an amount that is sufficient to settle the estate and pay outstanding business debts, the need to sell the business interest quickly in order to raise needed cash is eliminated.

Providing Interim Working Capital. The loss of the business owner often results in the tightening of business credit and supplier terms. Life insurance can provide the capital needed to continue business operations until the best possible price can be obtained either for its assets or for the business as a going concern. Without sufficient working capital during this tenuous period, it is more likely that the business will lose value rather than gain it.

Replacing Lost Business Value

To the extent that life insurance is used to pay estate settlement costs and provide interim working capital, it acts as a facilitator. Although that role is, unquestionably, important, its major role in the planned liquidation of a business interest, however, is its replacement of the value that will inevitably be lost as a result of liquidation.

When we think about liquidation of a business interest at the death of a business owner, we usually think about the liquidation of a sole proprietorship and, to a lesser extent, the liquidation of a partnership. Seldom do we think about the liquidation of a corporation. As pointed out earlier in our discussion, however, both corporations and incorporated businesses may face liquidation—and, largely, for the same reasons. So, when we consider the loss that liquidation occasions, we need to be aware of the loss sustained by three different groups:

1. the surviving members of the deceased business owner's family;

2. the remaining partners in a partnership that will be liquidated; and

3. the remaining co-stockholders in a corporation facing liquidation.

For all three groups, the liquidation of a business results in a substantial loss of business value. In almost every case, the business value will shrink when it is liquidated. Although the shrinkage may be inevitable, its effect on the family, partners and co-stockholders is not nearly so inevitable. Life insurance may help all three avoid that loss.

For the Heirs. In addition to the loss of the business value, the surviving family usually suffers the loss of its primary—and, sometimes, its only—income. While the successful business owner may have provided his or her family with many of the advantages that accompany wealth, the business owner's death may change that dramatically. However, the presence of life insurance can enable the family to remain in the world it knew before the death of the business owner. The advantages that inure to the heirs as a result of the appropriate use of life insurance in a sufficient amount on the life of the business owner are substantial.

- First, the heirs receive the entire value of the business, despite its erosion due to liquidation.

- Second, the insurance proceeds received by the heirs may avoid both probate costs and the claims of creditors.

- Third, any available life insurance proceeds can guarantee additional family income.

For the Remaining Partners and Co-Stockholders. The effect on the remaining partners and co-stockholders of the liquidated business can be almost as financially devastating as on the surviving family members. Not only do they face a substantial reduction in their assets, occasioned by the liquidation of the business, they will also lose their jobs and the income, benefits, satisfaction and security that came with them. In addition, for the partner, liquidation may have another consequence. If the partnership is in debt after collecting the accounts receivable, selling the assets and paying any debts, the surviving partner—because of his or her joint and several liability—may be liable for payment of any outstanding partnership liabilities.

These individuals may find it difficult to restart their careers, especially as they get older. In fact, it may be impossible for them to find any kind of appropriate employment. If they do find employment, how will they feel being *employees* rather than *employers?* Just as life insurance plays an important role for the surviving family members, it can also ease the burden that liquidation places on the shoulders of partners and co-stockholders.

Life insurance, owned by the remaining partners or co-stockholders on the life of the deceased business owner, can:

- replace the value lost on liquidation of the business;

- provide cash needed for a partner to pay off any remaining partnership liabilities;

- provide family income to help replace the income lost as a result of the loss of their jobs; and

- provide seed money for the possible starting of a new business.

Life insurance plays an important role for the surviving family members and the remaining partners or co-stockholders of the deceased business owner when the business is to be liquidated upon his or her death. What we will also see is that it plays an equally substantial role in the other two options: family retention and sale of the business as a going concern.

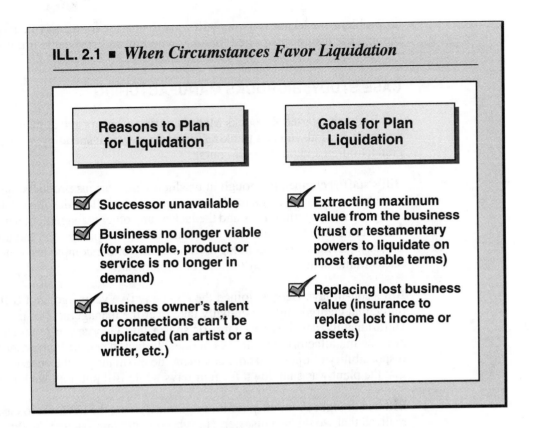

ILL. 2.1 ■ *When Circumstances Favor Liquidation*

Reasons to Plan for Liquidation

☑ Successor unavailable

☑ Business no longer viable (for example, product or service is no longer in demand)

☑ Business owner's talent or connections can't be duplicated (an artist or a writer, etc.)

Goals for Plan Liquidation

☑ Extracting maximum value from the business (trust or testamentary powers to liquidate on most favorable terms)

☑ Replacing lost business value (insurance to replace lost income or assets)

■ TAX AND ESTATE PLANNING ISSUES

We have seen that liquidation of a business interest can cause it to lose half or more of its value. Accounts receivable are compromised and business assets are sold at pennies on the dollar. For the surviving family, liquidation of a business may be a financial tragedy of major proportions. However, the business owner can address the important tax and estate planning issues before that happens so that liquidation of the business need not mean liquidation of the family's way of life.

Most of the time , the important estate planning issues involve the replacement for the survivors of both the income that the business produced and the lost value of the business itself. For many business owners and their families, the business is responsible for virtually all of the family's income. On the death, disability or retirement of the business owner, that income ceases and must be replaced if the family is to be able to continue its lifestyle. In the case of the business owner's death or disability, that family income may be replaced through the use of life and disability income insurance. If liquidation of the business is the result of the owner's retirement, a qualified retirement plan may be used to produce the needed income. Likewise, the value of the business may be replaced through the medium of life insurance.

The tax issues that may be important to resolve in the event of the business interest liquidation principally concern estate taxes. Because the business liquidation value is customarily low relative to its value as a going concern, the likelihood of income tax problems is not usually very great. If the estate value is expected to result in a tax problem, the business owner will want to provide for the payment of those taxes through life insurance applied for and owned by an irrevocable life insurance trust.

■ CASE STUDY: BIGBUCKS MANUFACTURING

Bill Bigbucks started Bigbucks Manufacturing 30 years ago at the age of 25. Now, at age 60, he finds himself thinking increasingly about spending more time with his grandchildren and on the golf course.

Bill's staff is competent enough in producing the various products the business manufactures, so the company has managed to stay afloat despite the falling off of many of the competing firms and the lack of any other management person to whom Bill could delegate some of the responsibilities. The problem in the industry is its increasing reliance on technology, which many of the companies—including Bigbucks Manufacturing—can't afford to implement.

Bill's son-in-law, George, joined the company five years ago, and Bill hoped, initially, that George might eventually take over the management of the business. Unfortunately, despite being a terrific son-in-law, George can't seem to understand how the manufacturing business operates. In fact, when Bill gave George the responsibility of operations management, he mismanaged the scheduling so badly that the plant was shut down for four days while Bill put it all back together.

Bill had thought about the possibility of transferring the business to George but has realized that would be a disaster. He subsequently approached the three remaining manufacturing firms in the industry to see if they would be interested in purchasing the business. When they realized that the plant would require substantial investment in order to introduce the current technology, they declined. There doesn't seem to be any alternative but to liquidate the firm when Bill retires or dies. He fears that a liquidation, however, would cost his family heavily.

Bill looked over the most recent balance sheet that the accountant had produced and added another column which he headed "Probable Value at Liquidation." Here is what Bill's calculations looked like when he was finished:

	Current Value as Ongoing Business	Probable Value at Liquidation
Equipment	$750,000	$100,000
Inventory	$150,000	$75,000
Accounts receivable	$200,000	$100,000
Other assets	$50,000	$20,000
Total balance sheet asset	$1,150,000	$295,000
Patents	$1,000,000	$500,000
Total assets	$2,150,000	$795,000

Liquidation means the almost-certain loss of $1,355,000 in company assets which, for Bill and his wife Beth, means their assets. In addition, upon Bill's death, the family's $250,000 income will also be lost.

Bill's thoughts turned to his and Beth's personal assets that she could use to help provide an income at his death. He decided to list them as well.

Assets		*Liabilities*	
Home	$575,000	Home mortgage	$225,000
Personal property	$75,000	Burial and final expenses	$10,000
Securities	$150,000	Estate administration	$50,000
IRA	$200,000	Policy loan	$25,000
Life insurance	$85,000	Other debts	$12,500
Business's liquidated value	$795,000	Inheritance tax	$20,000
Total	$1,880,000		$342,500

Bill's Concerns

Bill is convinced that the uncertainty of the future for Bigbucks Manufacturing—because of the costs involved in technological improvements coupled with the lack of any successor—makes business liquidation the only real alternative.

Bill is concerned about the loss of the business value that would happen at his death. He is even more concerned, however, with the loss of income that would result. Even though it appears from his calculations that Beth would inherit over $1.5 million, a large part of that inheritance is their home which wouldn't produce any income for Beth. In fact, after subtracting the value of the house and the various debts that would have to be paid, Beth would be left with $1,112,500 with which to produce income. That is only a little more than four times their current annual income.

If Beth invested the money at 7 percent, which Bill thought was reasonable, it would still only give her an income of $77,875—a long way from the $250,000 Beth was accustomed to. After talking with Beth, they agreed that she would need about 60 percent of their current income to continue to live as they were upon Bill's death. Bill calculated that he would need to find a way to provide an additional $72,125 of annual income for her.

The Solution

Bill realizes he needs to accomplish two important goals. The first goal is to minimize the value loss on liquidation of the business. The second goal is to ensure that Beth has sufficient income, which has been determined to be $150,000 yearly.

Because he intends to have his estate use the unlimited marital deduction, he antic-ipates that there will be no federal estate taxes due.

Bill scheduled a meeting with his insurance agent and attorney to discuss the options available to enable him to achieve both goals. In the meeting, Bill's attorney outlined various changes that will be required in Bill's will to ensure that his exec-utor is given the powers needed to liquidate the business at a time that is most likely to maximize its value. One of those provisions will hold the executor harmless in the event his exercise of the powers results in a loss of value to the heirs.

Bill's insurance agent has recommended a life insurance policy for $1,030,357 which will produce an additional $72,125 each year when invested at the 7 percent that Bill believes is reasonable. The agent has also recommended that the life insur-ance policy be purchased and owned by an irrevocable life insurance trust that can be created by the attorney.

By using the trust, the $1,030,357 of death benefit proceeds will not be included in Bill's estate at his death, and, more importantly, it will avoid inclusion in Beth's estate at her death. At Bill's death, the proceeds paid to the trust will be invested by the trustee and will provide an income to Beth for her lifetime. Upon Beth's death, the balance of the trust will be paid to Bill and Beth's daughter, Susan, and her hus-band George. The additional death benefits, which will escape estate taxes on both Bill's and Beth's deaths, will replace the lost business value caused by its liquidation.

The premiums for the life insurance owned by the trust will be paid through annual gifts made by Bill and joined into by Beth.

■ SUMMARY

In this chapter we examined the conditions that suggest liquidation as the appropri-ate course of action rather than family retention or sale for the departing business owner. We found that those conditions include the unavailability of competent suc-cessor management, the lack of interest on the part of the heirs in assuming business responsibilities, a lack of general business profitability, possible legal impediments and the inability to replace unique business owner talents or skills.

When liquidation is determined to be the appropriate course of action, it can be the result of inaction on the part of the business owner, or the liquidation can be planned and orderly. We examined the results of the owner's failure to plan for the liquida-tion and found that the failure resulted in a generally greater loss of value. Planned liquidation was addressed as the only viable means of minimizing the erosion of the business value. That planning enables the business owner to limit asset loss through the granting of important powers to his or her executor and to offset the loss through the purchase of life insurance.

The tax and estate planning issues that are important on liquidation of the business were identified and discussed. They include provision for replacing the asset value of the business, replacing the income that the business provided and arranging for life insurance—in an irrevocable life insurance trust, if appropriate—to pay any estate taxes due.

■ **CHAPTER 2 QUESTIONS FOR REVIEW**

1. What is the required disposition of a sole proprietorship upon the death of the business owner?

   A. It must be sold to employees.

   B. It must be retained by the family.

   C. It must be liquidated.

   D. It must be sold at auction as an ongoing business.

2. How soon after the death of a decedent are federal estate taxes generally payable?

   A. 60 days

   B. 90 days

   C. 6 months

   D. 9 months

3. Which of the following would NOT be a factor in favor of liquidation?

   A. Uninterested heirs

   B. High business profitability

   C. Non-transferable goodwill

   D. Substantial business risk

4. Which of the following is a requirement for ownership of stock in a professional corporation?

   A. Being licensed to practice the profession

   B. Agreement to assume liability for the professional actions of the other stockholders

   C. Permission of the licensing authority

   D. Agreement to make a minimum capital contribution of $25,000

5. Which of the following powers would NOT customarily be granted to the executor in order to promote the orderly liquidation of a business interest?

   A. Power to sell the business

   B. Power to retain the business

   C. Power to loan money from the business

   D. Power to change the organizational form

3

Family Retention of the Business

I t is not so unusual that a successful business owner would want to retain a business in the family and pass it along to the heirs at his or her death, disability or retirement. In addition to the hard work that probably accounts for its success, the business owner often has a large amount of ego tied up in it and may want to leave a successful business as a monument to that hard work.

Despite the wishes of the business owner, however, not every business is a suitable candidate for family retention. As we've seen, the circumstances that favor the retention of a business in the family include:

- *Successor management is available.* Although an heir is usually the most desirable successor manager, others, including current employees or outsiders, may be acceptable substitutes. Regardless of the identity of the successor, he or she should possess management skills, leadership ability, industry knowledge and knowledge of the operations of the business.

- *The business is profitable.* An unprofitable business seldom becomes profitable when a less-knowledgeable owner takes over. If the business is currently unprofitable, or if its future profitability is questionable, the business owner should reconsider any thoughts of its retention upon his or her death, disability or retirement.

- *The business is unsalable.* The fact that a business is one that is not easily sold may significantly affect its value upon its sale and, certainly, upon its liquidation. Although some unsalable businesses should not be retained, its unsalability as an ongoing business may make family retention more attractive.

- *There is a tradition of family ownership.* A long-term tradition of ownership by and identification with a specific family may bring with it customer loyalty, favorable terms from suppliers and a strong working relationship with a banking source. While these factors may not guarantee that a business will continue to enjoy success, their absence can make attainment of business success more difficult. Where there is a family ownership tradition, retention should be strongly considered.

Even though each of these factors suggests family retention in a specific case still doesn't ensure that the business will remain in the family or that it will thrive. The key ingredient in making that happen is planning for family retention.

Chapter Objectives

In this chapter, you will learn:

- what is needed to retain a successful business in the family upon the death, disability or retirement of a business owner;

- what, specifically, must be done to effect the business transfer to a family member and enhance the probability of the business' success;

- the needs of any business upon its transfer to other family members; and

- the tax and estate planning issues that must be addressed if the business is to be successfully retained in the family.

■ ■ ■ ■ ■

■ TRANSFER OF OWNERSHIP TO A FAMILY SUCCESSOR

The circumstances that call for the transfer of ownership to a family successor are, of course, the death, disability or retirement of the business owner. The owner may have spent many years making the business a success and, often, wants to have it continue as a success for his or her children and grandchildren. Helping to ensure that success is a principal function of succession planning. Let's look at what is needed to facilitate that succession.

Important Factors in Facilitating Family Succession

Although every factor that we will examine plays an important role in making the family-retained business a success, a key factor in ensuring that success lies in identifying a family member who is both willing to enter the business and capable of managing it. Although heirs interested in retaining the family business may certainly employ others to manage it, the most successful small businesses are usually those in which the owners play an active management and leadership role.

Identifying the Potential Successor. The process of selecting a suitable family member to lead the business upon the departure of the current owner begins with identifying at least one—and, preferably, more than one—candidate. The task of identifying the potential successor should begin just as early as possible and long before the business owner plans to step down. Although business owners may begin to address the issue of their successor only shortly before their retirement,* they

---

* According to a 1997 survey of family businesses conducted by Arthur Anderson and Mass Mutual, nearly one-third of CEOs that were planning retirement within the next five years had not selected a successor.

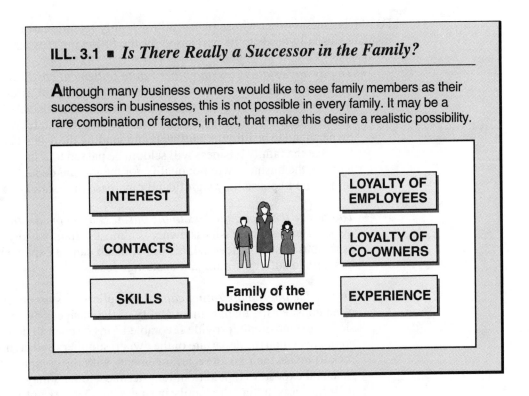

ILL. 3.1 ∎ *Is There Really a Successor in the Family?*

Although many business owners would like to see family members as their successors in businesses, this is not possible in every family. It may be a rare combination of factors, in fact, that make this desire a realistic possibility.

INTEREST

CONTACTS

SKILLS

Family of the business owner

LOYALTY OF EMPLOYEES

LOYALTY OF CO-OWNERS

EXPERIENCE

often fail to consider the possibility of their earlier departure from the business due to death or disability.

If the successor candidates are young and/or inexperienced, the business owner has an additional task. That task is one of identifying a non-family member who would be willing and capable of serving as an interim chief executive until one or more of the heirs are older and have gained sufficient experience to take over the business reins.

Changing Management Style. Both a hallmark and a major weakness of many family-owned and managed businesses is the owner's management style. This style can be characterized as the "manager as doer" rather than as delegator or teacher.

Since the selection of a successor requires that the candidate or candidates be both taught how to manage the business and tested to determine their ability, the business owner must forgo his or her characteristic doer style in favor of becoming the candidates' teacher and mentor. Of all the changes that may be called for, this one may be the most difficult because the owner has probably been accustomed to running the show entirely.

Adequate Life Insurance. Although the business owner may manage the business until his or her retirement—and often anticipates doing just that—there is no guarantee that he or she will live to do it. Purchasing an appropriate amount of life insurance is important regardless of the eventual disposition of the family-owned business. Its importance is even greater, however, when the business is to be retained by the heirs rather than sold or liquidated.

For the business owner whose plans call for family retention of the business, life insurance usually needs to be purchased for the following reasons:

- *To pay any estate taxes and other estate settlement costs.* Since the family business is often the business owner's most significant asset, life insurance must be purchased to avoid the requirement that the business be sold to meet estate liabilities. This is especially true because the estates of small business owners tend to be illiquid. Further compounding the estate tax problem is the fact that the family business will seldom be passed to a surviving spouse. As a result, the business will not qualify for the marital deduction, and its transfer to a non-spouse may significantly increase the estate's tax liability.

- *To replace the economic loss to the business upon the death of the business owner.* Because the business owner is almost certainly a key person insofar as the business is concerned, his or her death can be expected to cause the business to suffer a significant economic loss.

- *To provide interim operating capital.* Suppliers, customers and creditors often consider the management ability of the business owner in their decision to extend credit, provide favorable terms or even to do business with a company. Upon the departure of the owner, suppliers and creditors will often seek to revise their business arrangements with the company to limit their financial exposure. In addition, long-term customers may choose to spread their business among the family business competitors until they are certain that the business will continue as it had before the departure of the business owner. For the family business that may be reeling from the loss of its leader this means a temporary reduction in profits and the squeezing of cash flow. Without additional interim operating capital coming from life insurance, this temporary setback may result in an end to the business or at least serious hardship.

- *To equalize inheritance.* It is not unusual for only one child to work in and, eventually, take over the family business while the business owner's other children pursue different careers. Since the business is often the owner's most significant asset, this can result in an unintended and undesirable inequality of inheritance. Business owners will usually want to equalize the inheritance received by their children by purchasing life insurance to make up the difference.

- *To provide spousal and surviving family income.* During the period of ownership and active management by the business owner, the business may have provided most, if not all, of the family income. If the business is not to be owned by the surviving spouse upon the death of the business owner, a substitute for its income-providing ability must be found. Life insurance is usually the means through which the income for the spouse is replaced.

Adequate Disability Insurance.   While in any given year, one in 106 people die, one in eight will be disabled.* Disability insurance is often overlooked but provides

---

* Transactions, Society of Actuaries.

essential coverage for the business owner. In planning for family retention of the business, disability insurance enables the business owner:

- *To provide funds for the purchase of the business by the designated successor.* While the business owner's will can provide the necessary documentation to transfer the business upon his or her death, there is no comparable document, other than a buy-sell agreement, that accomplishes the same task when the owner becomes disabled. A separate but important benefit of disability insurance is that the determination of disability for purposes of activating the buyout is left to an impartial third party—the insurance company.

- *To provide income to the disabled business owner and his or her family.* Few businesses can afford to continue to pay the disabled business owner during an extended period of disability. Despite that inability to continue the business owner's salary, his or her expenses will usually increase during disability. As a result, the once-comfortable business owner may become deeply in debt. If the business chooses to continue to pay the business owner, the IRS may consider those payments—in the absence of a sick pay plan—to be nondeductible ad hoc benefits. If the company is organized as a corporation, it may deem them dividends.

- *To replace lost business earnings.* The disabled business owner may be as lost to the business as the deceased business owner. The consequences are generally the same: suppliers and creditors may revise their business arrangements with the company to limit their financial exposure; long-term customers may spread their business among competitors until they are certain that the business will continue as it had before the departure of the business owner. The family business may not survive these changes that result in lost earnings unless those earnings are replaced upon the business owner's disability. Key person disability coverage is designed to do just that.

Successor Training and Development. The appropriate development of the successor, as pointed out earlier, often requires that the business owner change his or her management style. The traditional doer must give way to the delegator and trainer. In other words, the entrepreneur must become a manager.

The principal function of the business owner in helping to assure the success of his or her successor lies in the successor's appropriate development. During this period, the successor candidate needs to learn about:

- the technical aspects of the business (i.e., its operations);

- the competition;

- the suppliers; and

- how to manage the business.

To ensure that this education is successful, the business owner must delegate meaningful business tasks to the identified successor *and let him or her make mistakes.* This requires that the entrepreneur overcome the natural tendency to jump in and correct the mistake. By correcting the successor's mistakes, however, he or she will miss the opportunity to learn by them.

It is almost certain that the successor will not manage the company in precisely the way the business owner did. However, the more time that the successor has to observe his or her predecessor and see what works and what doesn't work, the greater is the likelihood that the positive attributes of the entrepreneur's management style will be absorbed.

Selecting the Successor. It is no secret that parents sometimes see in their children abilities and talents that the children don't really possess. In selecting a successor to manage the family business, this tendency can be fatal.

There are many factors that qualify an individual to manage and lead a business. Those factors include knowledge, motivation, ambition, temperament and education. It should be clear that family connections alone won't be sufficient if the business is to be successful.

In assessing the qualifications of the successor candidate to manage the business, the business owner must apply the same kind of judgment and honesty that helped to make the business a success. That means that the business owner needs to reject the candidate who doesn't possess the ability to manage the business and keep it successful. For many entrepreneurs this is a particularly difficult job.

To render the task of assessing and selecting the appropriate successor easier and more objective, the business owner may want to establish an independent board of directors committee to provide input on the selection. In the event that the business operates without a board of directors, a management committee composed of company officers can fulfill the same task. In addition to aiding in selection, the committee may fulfill other important functions.

Members of the committee may serve as both role models and mentors for the successor and can help to provide a historic context for why certain things are done as they are in the company. Certainly, committee members may help in training and educating the successor as well as in instilling certain leadership traits and business discipline. Finally, if the business owner should die or become disabled before the successor is considered fully ready to take control, the committee can provide hands-on management of the business until the successor is ready.

Communicating the Successor Selection. Perception is sometimes as important as reality. Not only must an appropriate selection of a successor be made, but, to satisfy the company's various constituencies, the successor must have and appear to have the full support and confidence of the business owner. That involves communicating the selection and its support to company:

- employees

- shareholders

- suppliers

- bankers

- customers

A failure to communicate may be interpreted to mean that the business owner or company officials are withholding bad news. Since the selection of a successor who can help to guarantee that the business will continue to operate as it has is generally good news for everyone, that information should be shared completely. The results may be that:

- employee morale remains high and productivity increases as employees' fears of possible job loss are eased;

- shareholders feel their investment is safe and avoid becoming intimately involved in company management;

- suppliers, believing that business continuity is provided for, continue to provide credit and deliveries on favorable terms;

- bankers, satisfied that management has acted prudently and protected their investment, continue to offer appropriate credit; and

- customers continue their ordering patterns.

Now that we have looked at what is needed to facilitate business succession in the family-retained business, we need to examine the requirements more closely. Let's turn our attention to how, specifically, family retention of the business can be effected. For the balance of this section, we will concentrate on retaining the sole proprietorship. In the next section we will look at how the process of business retention differs depending upon the form of business organization.

Family Retention of the Sole Proprietorship

To avoid the unauthorized practice of law, it is important that competent legal counsel be brought into the business succession planning at an early stage. By doing that, you will not only avoid the appearance of practicing law, it will enable you to forge a working relationship with the business owner's attorney that will help you to get the planning job done with a minimum of difficulty.

There is a considerable amount of document drafting that must be accomplished to provide for the retention of a family business. This drafting is, of course, the province of the attorney. Because there are three contingencies that need to be provided for—death, disability and retirement of the business owner—the documents must address each of them.

Document Drafting to Facilitate Family Retention

Death. Not unexpectedly, perhaps, the document that addresses the planned retention of the business interest in the event of death is the business owner's will. It must contain provisions that give specific powers to the executor that will facilitate retention. Let's look at those provisions. The executor must be given:

1. the power to retain the business indefinitely;

2. the power to operate the business;

3. the power to change the form of the enterprise (i.e., from a sole proprietorship to a partnership, LLC or corporation if the change is prudent); and

4. the power to borrow against the estate's assets in order to provide estate liquidity to preserve the estate's assets.

In addition, the will must contain a provision that releases the executor from personal liability for his or her actions in carrying out the enumerated powers provided they were done in good faith and in the interests of the estate and its heirs.

Disability.   The document that must be drafted to ensure the transfer of ownership in the event of the business owner's disability is a *funded disability buyout agreement.* Although the business can be gifted by the disabled business owner rather than sold to the heir, an intended gifting strategy carries with it a number of concerns, including:

- uncertainty that the gift will actually be made upon disability;

- donor competence at the time a gift is made; and

- possible gift taxes to the extent that the value of the business exceeds the annual gift tax exclusion.

The funded disability buyout agreement performs a number of important functions including:

- setting the price that the disabled business owner will receive for the business;

- establishing the buyout terms (i.e., a lump-sum or payments over a period of time and at what disability duration the buyout would commence);

- referencing the funding vehicle (i.e., the disability insurance policy); and

- establishing the criteria for disability (i.e., the disability insurance policy's definition).

Retirement.   A transfer of the business interest during the business owner's lifetime can take one of two forms. It can involve either a sale or a gift, and the necessary documentation will depend, of course, upon which approach is chosen. While a simple outright sale or gift may require little explanation, there are specific approaches to gifting or selling that may be particularly suited to the intra-family lifetime transfer of a business interest that deserve discussion.

The decisional factors that often guide the choice of gift or sale to a family member and the specific approach to be employed are:

- a desire to give the business every opportunity to succeed;

- the business owner's possible need for income from the business during retirement; and

- a desire to avoid or minimize income, gift and estate taxes.

A sale of the business interest may be a simple one in which ownership of the business passes to the successor in return for a lump-sum payment (usually with funds borrowed from a lending institution) or installment payments to be made out of corporate cash flow. The concern, especially in a small family business, is that such an approach may cripple the company's operations by hampering its cash flow.

To some extent, this cash flow concern may be overcome through the use of two different approaches: the *private annuity* and the *self-canceling installment note* (SCIN). Because these approaches require competent counsel experienced in their use and are beyond the scope of this book, we will do little more than describe them and list their advantages.

The Private Annuity.   A private annuity is a vehicle through which appreciated property is often transferred to a family member in return for an unsecured promise to make fixed periodic payments for the remainder of the transferor's life. Since the promise is an unsecured one—a secured promise could result in adverse tax consequences—this method of property transfer is usually limited to those situations in which a close relationship of trust exists between the two parties to the transaction. The income generated by the family business is a major source—possibly the only funding source—of the annuity payments.

Although no strategy is without disadvantages in particular situations, the benefits of a private annuity are substantial. They include all of the following:

- The business owner will receive an income that he or she cannot outlive.

- Gift taxes are avoided, assuming the sale of the business interest in exchange for the private annuity is for a full and adequate consideration.

- Income taxes on the business sale are spread over a number of years, and no interest is assumed to be part of the periodic private annuity payments.

- The value of the business will not be included in the business owner's federal gross estate since a bona fide sale will remove it.

- No part of the value of the annuity will be included in the business owner's federal gross estate because the right to the annuity payments is extinguished at the business owner's death.

The Self-Canceling Installment Note (SCIN).   The self-canceling installment note can be characterized as a hybrid of a private annuity and a standard installment note that attempts to incorporate the advantages of both in a single instrument. It is sometimes referred to as a death-terminating installment sale. Like both the private annuity and the standard installment note, it is used for the sale of the business.

The SCIN is an installment obligation that calls for the periodic payment of a fixed amount over a specified period of time. Unlike the standard installment note, however, the obligation for payment ends at the earlier of the payment period specified in the note and the death of the payee. Because there is a possibility that the note will be extinguished by the death of the business owner before it ends by its terms, the business successor customarily pays a risk premium that may be stated as a higher sales price or as a higher-than-market interest rate. For a transaction involving a SCIN to be treated as a sale rather than one involving a gift, the consideration paid should reflect a bargained-for risk premium.*

The self-canceling installment note also provides some significant advantages and disadvantages. The SCIN advantages include all of the following:

- The business owner will receive an income from the transfer of the business; *however, the business owner may outlive the income if payments end by the terms of the note during his or her lifetime.*

- Gift taxes are avoided, as they were using the private annuity, assuming the sale of the business interest in exchange for the SCIN is for a full and adequate consideration.

- Unlike the private annuity, the SCIN may be secured without adverse tax consequences.

- Income taxes on the business sale are spread over a number of years; however, interest on the SCIN would be taxable to the business owner and generally deductible to the successor.

- The value of the business will not be included in the business owner's federal gross estate since a bona fide sale will remove it.

- No part of the value of the SCIN will be included in the business owner's federal gross estate because the right to continued installment note payments is extinguished at the business owner's death, just as it is in the case of the private annuity.

While the self-canceling installment note and the private annuity work well in those intra-family transfers involving a sale of the business, other intra-family transfers—especially those in which the business owner requires no additional retirement income from the sale—should be considered. These involve inter vivos gifting strategies. One of the most popular is known as a *grantor retained trust (GRT)*.

Grantor Retained Trust (GRT).   Under a grantor retained trust, a business owner may make a gift of a business interest into an irrevocable trust and retain an income from it. The income period may be for a term of years or for the lifetime of the grantor. The gift is considered a gift of a future interest and, accordingly, does not qualify for the annual gift tax exclusion. However, the value of the gift for gift tax purposes is determined by subtracting the value of the retained portion—the present value of the income stream to be received by the donor—from the present value of the gifted property. Accordingly, the greater the value of the retained income, the smaller the gift for purposes of gift tax liability.

Under current law, only specific trusts allow the donor business owner to subtract the value of his or her retained interest when the trust beneficiary is a family member. When valuing non-residence gifts in trust for family members the donor may

---

* Edwin T. Hood, et. al., *Closely Held Businesses in Estate Planning*, pp. 60-61.

reduce the gift tax value by the value of the retained income interest—which would normally reduce gift taxes if the trust is either an annuity trust or a unitrust.

Under a *grantor retained annuity trust (GRAT)*, which may be the more desirable of the two approaches from an estate tax perspective as well as from an expense viewpoint, the trust makes a periodic fixed payment to the grantor. Under a *grantor retained unitrust (GRUT)*, the trust makes a periodic payment of a fixed percentage of the value of the property in trust. At the end of the income period, the business along with any business appreciation is transferred to the trust beneficiary.

A significant disadvantage of the GRUT is the requirement that it be revalued each year. That revaluing generally requires a costly annual appraisal and, if the property has appreciated, a larger payment to the grantor that may increase the business owner's federal gross estate.

Using these gifting strategies, however, can produce a number of benefits for the business owner. Among those benefits are the following:

- The business owner will receive an income from the transfer of the business.

- Gift taxes are reduced because of the income interest retained by the business owner.

- The value of the business will not be included in the business owner's federal gross estate since it was not owned by him or her at death.

- No part of the value of unpaid periodic retained income payments will be included in the business owner's federal gross estate because the right to continued payments is extinguished at the business owner's death.

A significant disadvantage of these gifting strategies, when compared with strategies involving a sale of the business interest, concerns income taxes. Income taxes on the business sale are spread over a number of years and are reduced due to any cost basis the business owner had in the interest. In the case of a gifting strategy, however, the business owner's cost basis is transferred to the successor and any interest received by the business owner is fully income taxable.

Funding Family Retention of the Business Interest

The Role of Life Insurance

Regardless of the nature of the event that results in the need for succession in the case of a family-retained business interest, insurance funding is an important element in its facilitation. The orderly and efficient transfer of the business interest in the event of death, disability or retirement of the business owner requires that funds be available.

In the case of the death of the business owner, the business interest usually is passed through the last will and testament. As a result, no funds are required to fund its purchase. Funds required by the business should be provided by life insurance, owned by the business, to:

- replace the economic value of the deceased business owner for the business; and

- provide interim operating capital.

In addition, life insurance should be purchased and owned by an *irrevocable life insurance trust (ILIT)* to pay any estate taxes due upon the death of the business owner and provide income to the surviving family members. If taxes are due and there are insufficient assets in the estate, the business may have to be sold to pay them, despite any plans made to the contrary for family retention.

Finally, life insurance should be owned by non-inheriting children on the life of the business owner, if needed, to equalize the inheritance received by the children.

Because the life insurance required in this situation is designed to fund a non-temporary need, it should be of the permanent variety. In addition, the permanent life insurance owned by the business can be used to help fund the purchase of the firm in the event of the business owner's retirement.

The Role of Disability Insurance

Disability insurance is also needed, primarily for two purposes: to fund the buyout and to provide income. A disability insurance policy should be owned by the business and used to fund the disability buyout agreement. Although the premium payments on this policy will not be tax deductible, the payment made upon the disability of the insured will be received by the business tax free.

An additional disability policy should be owned by the business owner and purchased, either by the business owner or by the business, to provide replacement income for the business owner in the event of his or her disability. If the business is taxed as a regular corporation, the premium can be tax deductible to the business, but the disability benefit received by the business owner will be considered taxable income.

■ DIFFERENCES CAUSED BY TYPES OF ORGANIZATION

In this last section dealing with the retention of the business by the business owner's family, our discussion centered principally upon the sole proprietorship. Although many of the considerations apply equally to the general partnership and the corporation, there are certain differences that result from the business' form of organization. An obvious difference is that, unlike sole proprietorships or partnerships, corporations do not cease legal existence upon the death of a stockholder. It is this and other differences that arise from the type of organization that we will explore.

The Sole Proprietorship

Let's begin by looking at the principal characteristics of the sole proprietorship as a jumping-off point.

Business Type	Sole proprietorship
Characteristics	Simplest form to establish.
	No separate business entity apart from the individual.
	Individual may use a dba for the business to distinguish it.
Transferability	May be sold at any time by the sole proprietor.
	Sale of the business is deemed to be a sale of each of its assets; gain or loss is computed for each asset individually.
	At the sole proprietor's death, without a written plan, business assets must be converted to cash as quickly as possible.
Income Taxation	Complete flow-through of income to individual.
	Business tax return filed as part of individual's tax return.
Owner Liability	Complete personal liability.
Existence	Business dies with the death of the sole proprietor.

When it comes to family retention of the business, the most important fundamental difference arises out of the fact that in the sole proprietorship there is only one owner. In fact, for many purposes, the sole proprietor and the business are the same entity. The business taxation is really just a part of the business owner's taxation. The assets of the business owner are fully attachable to satisfy the debts of the business.

Although the identification of the business with the business owner has certain drawbacks, such as unlimited liability, it also has certain strengths, depending on the goals of the owner. Singular ownership permits the greatest amount of flexibility in retaining the business in the family. There are no partners whose consent is required or co-stockholders who could block the heirs' active participation in the business. As we will see, the partnership and close corporation may present some formidable obstacles to family retention.

The General Partnership. As we discussed in Chapter 1, an effective general partnership often is the result of a unique intermarriage of the talents and abilities of the individual partners. The partnership, when it works especially well, is synergistic in that the total of the efforts of the individuals produces a greater result than the simple sum of those efforts.

The closeness of partners and the general partnership is reflected in the liability each of the partners assumes by joining the general partnership. This is referred to as joint and several liability. This liability makes the personal assets of the partners, including their savings, automobiles and homes—as well as the partners' investment in the partnership—subject to attachment to meet the debts of the partnership.

It is largely because of this assumption of liability for the actions of the other partners that the partnership form with its existing partners is entirely voluntary. In other words, no one can require an individual to be another's partner or to remain in a partnership whose partners have changed. For this reason, in the absence of a written agreement to the contrary, partnerships die with the death of a partner.

Family retention of the partnership interest, accordingly, requires the consent of all of the partners. For this reason, liquidation is the normal consequence of the death of a partner unless provisions have been made to avoid it.

If the remaining partners of the deceased business owner and his or her heirs do not wish to liquidate the organization, and the heirs don't wish to sell their interest to the remaining partners, only two alternatives are available. Both of those alternatives involve the reorganization of the partnership. The alternatives are as follows:

- the remaining partners take the heirs into the partnership as partners; or

- the heirs buy out the remaining partners.

In either approach, there are sizable concerns.

The characteristics of the general partnership are shown as follows.

Business Type	General partnership
Characteristics	An association of two or more persons who organize to carry on business for a profit.
	Partnership agreement need not be written.
	Business is managed by the partners who *generally* have an equal voice in running it.
Transferability	Any change in a partnership creates a new firm.
	New partners may not be brought into the firm without the consent of each existing partner.
	Partners may not sell their partnership interest without the consent of each existing partner.
	Death of any partner automatically dissolves the partnership absent a written agreement to the contrary.
Income Taxation	Partnership files an information tax return.
	Income is passed through to the partners for income tax purposes.
Owner Liability	Partners have joint and several liability.
	Each partner is personally liable for the debts of the business and the business actions of other partners.
Existence	Absent a written plan, surviving partners become liquidating trustees upon the death of any partner.
	The partnership does not survive the death of a partner.

As we can see from the chart above, each partner is personally liable for the expenses and debts of the partnership, and both the contractual and negligent actions of the partners in their role as partners is attributable to each of the other partners.

Heirs Become Partners. The first impediment to this approach is that both the heirs and the remaining partners would be required to agree to reorganize the partnership to include the heirs before the reorganization could go forward. The refusal of any partner is sufficient to derail the possible reorganization. Let's consider why, despite the loss that follows upon liquidation, a partner might be unwilling to enter into a partnership with the deceased partner's heirs.

We began this section with a discussion of why individuals choose to become partners, and saw that the reason frequently was principally to engender a certain synergism whereby each partner's contribution is magnified by the contributions of the other partner or partners. If we consider how rare it is to find someone whose abilities, talents and personality mesh so completely with our own that the combined result of our efforts is greater than the sum of our individual results, it's easy to understand why the remaining partners' taking the heirs into the business as partners often doesn't work. Such a reorganization may occasionally be satisfactory, but that is usually the exception. Consider the following possible impediments to taking the heirs into the partnership organization:

- Although the deceased partner may have had exceptional general business skills, his or her heirs may have little or no business acumen.

- The heirs may fail to possess the interpersonal skills that would permit them to work harmoniously with the remaining partners.

- The departed partner's special contribution to the business may have been the result of his or her contacts with customers, relationships with credit sources or other talent, skill or relationship; the heirs may not be able to replace that special contribution.

- There may be a legal impediment to the heirs' becoming partners because they may not possess special professional licensing possessed by the former partner.

We have been assuming in our discussion that the heirs would become active partners in the organization. That arrangement is not the only one in which heirs could become partners in the organization. They could become inactive partners—sometimes referred to as "silent" partners. Not unexpectedly, this arrangement also involves substantial concerns.

The first concern is that silent partners seldom remain silent. Because the heirs as inactive partners would receive income from the partnership only to the extent that it produced a profit, they may believe that the active partners were failing to maximize the business profitability and attempt to interfere in its management. If permitted to affect the course of the business, their need to maximize current income could conflict with a business growth strategy being implemented by the active partners.

Inactive partners also present another concern for the partnership. They normally continue to be paid the same percentage as the departed partner. Since the departed partner probably made an important contribution to the partnership, the remaining partners may need to hire a replacement. This will increase the partnership expenses and, accordingly reduce its profitability, and will reduce the income to both the active partners and the silent partners. The active partners may feel—and rightly so—that they are putting forth the entire effort and having to split the profits. The silent partners, because of a reduction in their income, are likely to become far less silent.

Selling the Partnership to the Heirs.   The other reorganization possibility, of course, is for the remaining partners to sell their interest to the heirs. Unless the heir or heirs were working in the partnership at the time of the business owner's departure and enjoyed the full confidence and support of the other partners, this is usually the only viable option for keeping the partnership interest in the family. Let's look at this approach.

The heirs' buying the remaining partners' interests in the business usually works best only when the deceased partner possessed a majority share of the partnership. Although the remaining partners—or even one of the remaining partners—could refuse to sell his or her interest, the likelihood of that happening is not great because the consequence would likely be that the partnership would be liquidated, and the remaining partners would be out of a job. By selling to the heirs, the remaining partners may be able to remain employed.

The primary problem in the remaining partners' selling their partnership interests to the heirs is that the heirs may not possess the ability to make the business successful. In addition, it may be unlikely that the former partners (assuming they had sold their interests to the heirs) would have the same level of dedication to the business that they possessed when they were owners. Furthermore, the former partners may be unable or unwilling to acclimate to their role as employees instead of employers and may leave the organization to begin a new—and, possibly, competing—business.

The Corporation.   Let's turn our attention to family retention when the business organization is a corporation. Again, before we do that, consider the important characteristics of the corporation that are shown in the chart below.

Business Type	Corporation
Characteristics	Most formal of the three basic organizational forms.
	Business has a completely separate tax and legal personality apart from its owners.
Transferability	Ownership is represented by stock shares that are freely transferable. (In a close corporation, stock transfer is often restricted.)
Income Taxation	Business is a separate tax entity. It files and pays its own state and federal income taxes without regard to the tax status of its stock holders.

Owner Liability   In the absence of fraud or other special circumstances, stockholders are not personally liable for the corporation's debts. Their liability is limited to their investment in the business.

Existence   Legally, corporations enjoy perpetual existence. The death of a stock holder does not affect the legal status of the business.

When we speak of retaining the corporate business interest in the family, we are referring to the heirs playing an active role in the management of the company's operations similar to that played by the departed business owner. We are not referring to *inactive* ownership of the corporate stock.

For purposes of family retention of the corporate business interest, the two most important characteristics of the corporation are:

- the easy transferability of stock; and

- the corporation's perpetual legal existence.

Unless the business is one that requires specific state licensure to be an owner, such as a physician, attorney or CPA who is a stockholder in his or her professional corporation, shares of corporate stock pass freely to heirs just as any other property would. Those are the principal legal aspects concerning family retention of the corporate business interest. In addition, it is important that the corporate business interest that is to be retained in the family be a majority interest.

There are, however, practical (rather than legal) issues with respect to family retention of the corporate business interest that are strikingly similar to the practical issues concerning family retention of the partnership or sole proprietorship. In fact, many close corporations are really operated as nothing more than incorporated sole proprietorships or partnerships and, accordingly, face many of the same concerns. Those practical issues include:

- the availability of a competent successor manager who can, within a reasonable time, pick up where the departed business owner left off;

- the continued provision of credit and delivery terms from bankers and suppliers; and

- acceptance by the business' principal customers of the new business owner.

If the business interest is less than a majority interest or if any of these issues cannot be answered in the affirmative, the chances of success in the family retention of the corporate business interest are compromised.

Estate Liquidity.   The requirement that the business owner's estate have sufficient liquidity to meet estate settlement costs is as important for the corporate business interest as it is for the partnership or sole proprietorship. Without sufficient liquidity the estate may be forced to sell the corporate business interest, regardless of the wishes of the business owner or his or her heirs. The corporate business owner, however, has an option that is not available to others.

In the case of the corporate business interest, a non-total redemption of shares of corporate stock may be made in an amount equal to the sum of the costs to settle the estate without being considered a dividend provided there is sufficient corporate surplus to effect the redemption. In addition, because of the step-up in cost basis to the value on the date of death, the redemption can usually be made without incurring any capital gains taxes. This redemption is authorized by Section 303 of the Internal Revenue Code. Accordingly, it is known as a Section 303 stock redemption.

Because a stock redemption can usually be made only from funds in corporate surplus, it is important that life insurance, owned and paid for by the corporation in an amount sufficient to fund the redemption, be maintained by the company. That will ensure that sufficient funds will always be available to redeem the stock without the requirement that large amounts of corporate surplus be tied up. Although the premium for the life insurance coverage will not be deductible to the corporation, the death benefit, payable to the corporation, will be received income tax free.

Adequate Survivor Income and Sufficient Assets.   In the case of the active family retention of a business interest, the interest normally is left to a son or daughter—or at least to a family member other than the spouse. To ensure that the surviving spouse, if any, is not able to frustrate the plans for family retention of the business, it is important to provide adequately for him or her.

Because the spouse can generally elect against the will to obtain a share of the spousal assets at least equal to the statutory share, providing for the transfer of sufficient assets to the spouse may forestall a legal challenge to the will that could result in a forced sale of the business interest. In addition, providing sufficient income to the surviving family members (including the spouse) will tend to obviate calls for a dividend distribution from the corporation.

■ THE NEEDS OF THE BUSINESS

Up to this point, we have been talking mostly about the needs of the surviving family and the appropriate planning that must be done by the business owner to ensure that his or her business can be retained by the family. Let's shift our focus slightly to a consideration of the requirements of the business if it is to initially survive the departure of the business owner and, ultimately, prosper under the management of the family successor.

The principal needs of the business can generally be summed up by the four "C"s of business success: cash, competence, credit and customers. We should begin with a consideration of one of the most important of the four and the easiest to provide for—cash.

The Need for Cash

Survival of a small business is generally far less a function of profit than it is of cash flow. A profitable business without sufficient cash may soon find itself out of business. A cash-rich business, even if initially unprofitable, can often buy time to turn the corner and become profitable.

A business that finds itself without the services and presence of an important business owner—whether due to his or her death, disability or retirement—may have an enormous need for cash. Cash is absolutely necessary during this period to:

- reimburse the business for the economic loss it has sustained or will sustain because of the loss of a key person, the business owner;

- buy out other business owners, if necessary, whether they are partners or co-stockholders; and

- provide interim working capital. Because suppliers and other credit sources may tighten credit terms following the death of a trusted contact, it is essential that sufficient additional working capital be infused in order to enable the company to continue operating despite any unfavorable change in credit availability.

The Need for Competence

Survival of the business and its ultimate profitability depend, in large measure, on the competence of the successor to the business owner. The ideal successor will have been a part of the business during the lifetime of the business owner and will have undertaken meaningful projects in each of its important departments. As a result, the successor will have a working-level understanding of the business and its operations. The successor will also have had an opportunity to demonstrate his or her grasp of the business and its requirements.

In addition to having gained an important understanding of how the business operates and its challenges, working in the business will have exposed the successor to its employees. As a result of that exposure, employees may feel less concern for the company and their future when the successor takes the company reins.

Unfortunately, it is not always possible to find and develop the ideal successor. Often, the successor has little company experience and may need to acquire important management skills before being relied on to lead the company. When that is the case, it is vitally important that the business have a particularly competent second-in-command who can help guide the successor until he or she has acquired sufficient skills and experience. If that needed individual is not currently employed by the company, every effort should be made to locate him or her.

Not only is a talented back-up needed for the inexperienced successor, but the business also will need additional cash. That additional cash will usually be needed to locate the back-up if he or she is not currently an employee and will help to offset the economic loss to the company of the inevitable missteps of the not-yet-ready successor.

The best answer to the need for a competent successor, of course, is in locating and developing a successor candidate far in advance of the time when the successor will be needed to run the company. Development of the successor would include an understanding of the technical aspects of the business, the competition, the company's suppliers and how to manage the business. When it, then, becomes time for the successor to accede to the role, he or she will be ready.

The Need for Credit

Most businesses run on credit. It may be credit from bankers or from suppliers. But, regardless of the credit source, its availability may be the difference between a prosperous business and one that closes its doors.

Disregarding, for the moment, the critical role of credit in the expansion of a business, credit is needed for two important functions. Those two important functions are:

- the funding of inventory; and

- smoothing out cash flow "bumps."

Firms seldom "own" their inventory in the sense of using retained earnings to purchase it. Instead, they often rely on favorable credit terms from their suppliers and hope for revenue from inventory sales to pay for it. When that credit isn't available, the inventories maintained by many firms are necessarily reduced. As a result, sales that would normally be made because of the customer's immediate need and the availability of the goods are often lost because the product must be ordered from the supplier instead of being immediately available. The loss of sales further exacerbates any cash flow problems and reduces the firm's profitability.

Maintaining adequate cash flow is a perennial problem for many small businesses. Rent, payroll, utilities and all of the other usual expenses of running a business must be met despite mounting accounts receivable and customers who fail to pay on time. Ensuring that these expenses are paid on time often means that the firm's banker must extend additional credit.

The availability of credit requires that creditors—suppliers and other credit sources—be comfortable with the firm's:

- cash position

- management competence

- collateral

From the business owner's and succession planner's perspective, those credit requirements cry out for the need for immediate successor selection and development and for the maintenance of appropriate permanent life insurance and disability coverage.

The Need for Customers

Nothing happens until somebody sells something. That is as true for the small business as it is for AT&T or IBM. The big difference in the small firm, because of its more modest capitalization and revenue, is that the effects of customer loss are felt far sooner.

With the departure of a successful business owner, it is almost inevitable that the business will lose some customers. These may be customers whose business was entirely dependent upon the special personal relationship that was maintained with the business owner. While regrettable, these losses should be expected. The bigger challenge lies with the other customers, those whose patronage was not dependent upon the personality of the business owner.

Customers must believe that their requirements will continue to be met under the management of the successor. For this reason, the successor must become familiar with the firm's key customers and their needs. The best time for the successor to get to know the key accounts and for them to become familiar with him or her is during the successor's early development period while the business owner is still managing the firm and there is little concern about the loss of the customer. If, for some reason, that mutual getting-acquainted period cannot be done during the development period, it should be one of the first jobs to be undertaken by the successor.

■ TAX AND ESTATE PLANNING ISSUES

Guaranteeing Sufficient Estate Liquidity

The most significant tax and estate planning issue for the business owner who wants to retain the successful business in the family lies in ensuring that there is sufficient estate liquidity to meet the tax and other settlement expenses. The issue of estate and inheritance taxes may be as significant for the married business owner as it is for the unmarried business owner.

In most cases, the business will not pass to the surviving spouse upon the business owner's death. That means that the business interest will not qualify for the marital deduction, and the estate will, as a result, incur a higher estate tax liability. If there is insufficient estate liquidity to pay the taxes due, the business interest may have to be sold in order to create that needed liquidity. The answer is to create the needed liquidity beforehand to avoid having to sell.

If the business that is to be retained is an unincorporated business, the required liquidity can be best provided through the use of an *irrevocable life insurance trust (ILIT)*. The trust is established during the business owner's lifetime and exists solely to purchase life insurance. The premium for the life insurance is usually paid through annual gifts made by the business owner and, if the business owner is married, his or her spouse.

Upon the death of the business owner, the life insurance proceeds are paid to the trust, and the trustee uses the death benefit proceeds to loan money to the estate or purchase assets from it. The cash thus paid to the estate is then available to pay estate taxes and to meet other settlement expenses, such as probate costs, attorney's fees, executor's fees, etc. An important consideration that makes the use of the ILIT highly favored by estate planning practitioners is that the death benefit proceeds paid to the trust are not included in, and, therefore, do not increase, the business owner's estate.

As discussed earlier in this chapter, the corporate business owner may have an option for payment of estate settlement costs that is not available to owners of unincorporated businesses. That option is the Section 303 stock redemption.

A redemption of shares of corporate stock may be made in an amount equal to the sum of the costs to settle the estate. Even though the stock redemption is for less than the entire interest, it will not be considered a dividend provided certain requirements are met. Because a stock redemption can usually be made only from corporate surplus, life insurance, owned and paid for by the corporation in an amount sufficient to fund the redemption, should be maintained by the company.

To qualify for the non-dividend treatment of a stock redemption under Section 303, certain conditions must be met. Those conditions are as follows:

- The stock that is to be redeemed must be includible in the deceased business owner's federal gross estate.

- The stock value of all of the stock of the redeeming corporation that is includible in the deceased business owner's federal gross estate must exceed 35 percent of the decedent's adjusted gross estate.

- The amount that may be paid out by the corporation under the Section 303 stock redemption may not be more than the sum of:

  - all estate and inheritance taxes (including any generation-skipping transfer tax and state taxes) attributable to the business owner's death; and

  - funeral and administrative expenses allowed as an estate deduction.

Protection from Spouse's Election Against the Will

As we noted above, in the case of the active family retention of a business interest, the business is usually left to a son or daughter instead of to the spouse. In order to ensure that the surviving spouse, if any, is not able to frustrate the plans for family retention of the business, it is important to leave sufficient assets to him or her.

The surviving spouse's ability to elect against the will in order to obtain a share of the spousal assets at least equal to his or her statutory share could result in a frustration of the business owner's succession plans. By providing for the transfer of sufficient assets to the spouse a legal challenge to the will that could result in a forced sale of the business interest might be averted.

Providing Sufficient Income

The business owner must also be sure to make provision for enough income payable to the surviving family members. By providing sufficient income to the family, including the surviving spouse, the business owner may allow the business to avoid calls for payment from the company—a dividend distribution from a corporation or some other payment from the non-incorporated entity.

Equalizing the Inheritance

Many business owners are committed to treating their children equally in their inheritance, despite the fact that not all of the children may work in the business. This is an estate planning issue that can be easily resolved through the application of life insurance on the life of the business owner.

Because the value of a family-owned business often constitutes the bulk of a business owner's estate, leaving that business to one child may result in other children receiving a significantly smaller inheritance. An irrevocable life insurance trust can be used to purchase life insurance on the business owner's life, making the other children beneficiaries of the trust. The net result is the equalization of the children's inheritance without increasing the business owner's federal gross estate and, as a result, the estate's tax burden.

Avoiding Family Attribution Problems

When the corporate family business is to be retained in the family upon the departure of the business owner, there may be a problem of family attribution that could result in any redemption of stock being deemed a dividend distribution. If the business owner's transfer of ownership in a family-owned corporation includes the redemption of his or her stock, and unredeemed shares of stock are owned by the redeemed owner's spouse, children, grandchildren or parents, the possibility of family attribution is a real one. If the stock redemption strategy is important, the answer to the problem may lie in the business owner's (or his or her estate's) qualifying for a waiver of the family attribution rules by agreeing not to acquire stock in the corporation for at least 10 years.

■ CASE STUDY: BIGBUCKS MANUFACTURING

Two years ago, at age 60, Bill Bigbucks had anticipated that, upon his death or retirement as president of Bigbucks Manufacturing, the business would have to be liquidated. There was no heir who was interested in taking over the business, and the costs to update the technology were considered too substantial. As a result, Bill's will was changed to give the executor the needed powers to maximize the liquidated value, and an irrevocable life insurance trust had been established which owns a life insurance policy on Bill's life in the amount of $1,030,357.

In the intervening two years, a number of changes occurred. Bill's daughter, Susan, joined the business after raising her children, and has shown herself to have inherited some of her father's entrepreneurial ability. She has learned the manufacturing and is currently managing the company's manufacturing operations. In addition, Susan has expressed a desire to take over the business when her father retires or dies.

Susan's grasp of the manufacturing operations has resulted in the company's making significant technological advances, and Bigbucks Manufacturing's competitive position has improved substantially. Bill is thinking that his earlier plans for liquidation of the business should be changed so that the business can be taken over by Susan.

Bill looked at the company's balance sheet to see what such a change in plans would mean. The balance sheet showed the following financial information:

	Current Value
Equipment	$750,000
Inventory	$150,000
Accounts receivable	$200,000
Other assets	$50,000
Total balance sheet asset	$1,150,000
Patents	$1,000,000
Total assets	$2,150,000

Bill then re-worked his personal balance sheet. That looked as follows:

Assets		Liabilities	
Home	$575,000	Home mortgage	$225,000
Personal property	$75,000	Burial and final expenses	$10,000
Securities	$150,000	Estate administration	$50,000
IRA	$200,000	Policy loan	$25,000
Life insurance	$85,000	Other debts	$12,500
Business's liquidated value	$2,150,000	Inheritance tax	$565,000
Total	$3,235,000		$887,500

Bill's Concerns

Bill is delighted that his daughter, Susan, will be taking over the firm upon his death. However, her succeeding Bill changes the financial picture substantially. Most significantly, since the business would be willed to Susan upon Bill's death, it will not qualify for the marital deduction and will result in an additional $545,000 in estate taxes. Furthermore, since the business will be owned by Susan, its liquidated value, estimated to be $795,000, will not be available to help provide the income of $150,000 for Bill's wife Beth—as it would have been if the business had been liquidated.

The Solution

The additional estate taxes that would have to be paid at Bill's death will result in all of Bill and Beth's liquid assets being used to pay the $662,500 in taxes and other liabilities. In addition, since there is only $435,000 in liquid assets in the estate, the irrevocable life insurance trust will have to loan the balance—$227,500—to the estate to pay its liabilities. As a result, the trust will be reduced to $802,857. At 7 percent, the trust can be expected to produce an income for Beth of only $56,200. Accordingly, the trust will purchase an additional life insurance policy on Bill's life for $1,340,000 which, at 7 percent, will produce the balance of the $150,000 of income that Beth needs at Bill's death.

An additional life insurance purchase of $1 million will be made by the business to replace the economic loss to the business in the event of Bill's death before retirement. In addition, at Bill's retirement, the policy's cash value can be used as a down payment on the buyout by Susan of Bill's business interest.

The balance of Bill's interest will be purchased by Susan using a private annuity. By using this approach, Bill will receive an income for his lifetime, and Susan will receive the entire business interest. In addition, no further payments will be required upon Bill's death. Beth's income will be provided by the life insurance purchased by the irrevocable life insurance trust.

■ SUMMARY

In this chapter we looked at planning for the retention of the business in the business owner's family and evaluated those steps necessary to facilitate that retention. Those important steps include the identification of a successor, his or her development through the assignment of important management tasks and the purchase of life and disability income insurance to ensure the reaching of various personal and business goals.

Alternate strategies designed to transfer the business interest at retirement were discussed. They include the use of a private annuity, a self-canceling installment note, a grantor retained trust and a family limited partnership. In addition, the needs of the business were addressed. Those needs include the need for cash, competence, credit and customers. We then examined those steps that can be taken to ensure them.

Finally, we examined the tax and estate planning issues encountered when the business is to be retained in the family. These issues include guaranteeing the liquidity of the estate, protecting against a possible spousal election against the will, providing sufficient family income, equalizing the inheritance and avoiding possible family attribution problems.

■ CHAPTER 3 QUESTIONS FOR REVIEW

1. Which of the following forms of business is generally the simplest to establish?

   A. Corporation

   B. Sole proprietorship

   C. Partnership

   D. Limited liability company

2. What is the income period provided by a private annuity?

   A. Lifetime

   B. 10 years

   C. 20 years

   D. 30 years

3. In which of the following strategies is the promise of payment to the business owner unsecured?

   A. Installment note sale

   B. SCIN

   C. Private annuity

   D. Grantor retained trust

4. What happens to installment payments under a SCIN when the seller dies?

   A. The present value of the remaining payments is due within 90 days.

   B. The remaining payments are canceled.

   C. The remaining payments are continued to the heirs.

   D. The remaining payments are aggregated and provide the consideration for an annuity to the spouse, if any.

5. Under what circumstances may partners be required to accept the heirs of a deceased partner into the business?

   A. When the deceased partner owned a majority interest

   B. When the heirs request to become partners

   C. When the partnership is a professional partnership

   D. Never

4

Transferring a Business to Owners or Employees

I n earlier chapters, we examined the advantages, disadvantages and factors that favor both family retention of the business and its dissolution through liquidation. Although either liquidation or family retention may be indicated in any particular situation, the most desirable option for all parties in most cases hasn't yet been discussed. That option involves the transfer of the business to those individuals who are most familiar with and capable of running it—its other owners or, in some cases, its employees.

Many times the family has few business-related objectives other than replacing the income that the business provided during the business owner's active involvement in it. That singular objective may cause them to take business actions and pursue strategies that result in missed opportunities and a general deterioration of the business. Furthermore, business acumen is not hereditary.

The successful business owner, capable of leading others and adept at handling the day-to-day challenges of managing a business, probably developed those important skills through experience, education and motivation. They may not reside in his or her offspring.

When the business owner's family is interested primarily in providing a continuing income for itself and another owner in the business or an employee is interested in becoming an owner, the business owner should think in terms of business transfer instead of family retention or liquidation. That's the issue that this chapter will address.

Chapter Objectives

In this chapter, you will learn:

- those factors that favor transfer of the family business rather than its retention by the family or liquidation;

- the methods generally available to effect transfer of the business interest;

- the differences in required planning that result from the different types of business entities;

- the practical needs of the business to replace the key person and the economic loss suffered by the organization; and

- the tax and estate planning issues that must be addressed when the business is to be transferred to other owners or employees.

■ ■ ■ ■ ■

■ TRANSFERRING OWNERSHIP TO SUCCESSORS

Although many business owners dream of keeping the business interest in the family, sometimes that dream shouldn't become reality. Several factors favor the transfer of a business interest outside of the family. These include:

- the decedent's interest being a minority interest;

- no heirs being available to take over the business interest; and

- the availability of a buyer for the interest.

The good will that may exist between business owners, whether they are partners or co-stockholders, is one of those elements that enables the business to produce a result that is greater than the simple sum of its parts. That's called synergism, and the best businesses seem to have it in abundance.

Unfortunately, it is that good will that sometimes causes business owners to eschew formal succession documentation in favor of a verbal agreement. When that happens and a handshake replaces the written agreement, disaster sometimes lurks in the wings. The only way to be sure that ownership transfer occurs in the way that it is planned by the business owners is to have a funded buy-sell agreement.

The Buy-Sell Agreement in General

The agreement referred to as a buy-sell agreement is the written formalization of a mutual understanding between a willing buyer and a willing seller of a business or profession. In the written agreement, the intended buyers of the business interest agree to buy it and the intended sellers of the business interest agree to sell it upon the occurrence of one or more specific events, such as the death, disability or retirement of one of the business owners.

To ensure that the agreement is fulfilled, each of the parties to the agreement also agrees not to dispose of his or her business interest to anyone without first offering it to the other parties to the agreement. Although the purchase of insurance on the lives of the owners—both life and disability insurance—makes incredible sense as a manner of funding the business interest purchase, it is not required. There are several major commitments that each of the individuals makes in agreeing to and signing the buy-sell agreement. Let's examine the nature of those commitments.

ILL. 4.1 ■ *Letting Someone Else Take Over the Business*

The fact that no one in the family is willing or able to take over the business does not mean that the family is left out of the wealth of the business when the owner dies. Proper planning ensures that the maximum value can be preserved for the family while ensuring that nonfamily successors can continue the business profitably.

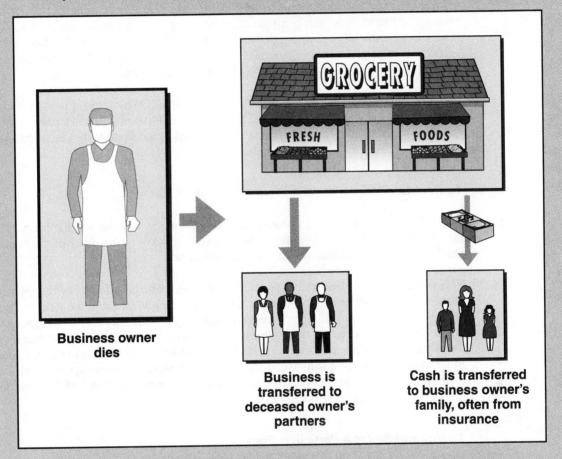

**Business owner
dies**

**Business is
transferred to
deceased owner's
partners**

**Cash is transferred
to business owner's
family, often from
insurance**

Commitments in the Buy-Sell Agreement

Simply from the name of the agreement, we can guess the first two commitments that are made in a buy-sell agreement. Someone agrees to buy, and someone agrees to sell.

To Buy

The remaining business owners—remember, they may be partners or co-stockholders—or the business itself must agree to purchase the business interest upon the occurrence of the triggering event; a triggering event would normally be the death, disability or retirement of the business owner.

To Sell

The business owner agrees to sell his or her business interest in the event of disability or retirement and commits his or her estate to sell the business interest in the event of death.

There are two basic approaches to the buy-sell agreement. The seller, of course, is the same in both approaches. The seller is the disabled, retired or deceased business owner, making the commitment either for him- or herself or on behalf of his or her estate. The buyer, however, is different, depending upon the approach chosen. The buyer may be the other partners or stockholders. When that approach is taken, the agreement is known as a *cross-purchase agreement* because each owner makes cross promises to buy or to sell as the circumstances warrant.

In the second approach, the buyer is the business itself. When this approach is chosen, the agreement is known as an *entity agreement* if the business is a partnership; it is a *stock redemption* if the business is organized as a corporation. Let's continue to look at the important commitments.

To Restrict Sale

Each of the owners makes a commitment that he or she will not sell the business interest during his or her lifetime without first offering it to the other partners or stockholders or to the business if it is a corporation.

This provision of the buy-sell agreement should call for the offering of the interest to the other owners or the corporation at the price recited in the agreement before selling it to an outsider. If the proposed outside buyer of the interest would agree to buy it only at a lower price, the business interest should be offered to the other owners or the corporation at that lower price before the sale can be made to the outsider. In addition to providing some security to the other business owners, the provision is important if the value set in the agreement is to be accepted by the IRS as the fair market value for federal estate tax purposes.

To Buy and Sell at a Particular Price

An agreement to buy or sell a business interest is of little value unless the agreement also states the price at which the interest will be bought or sold. The price at which the transaction will take place must be stated or determinable.

The simple method of handling the transaction price for the business interest is to state it in the agreement. For example, the agreement can contain a statement that the company share value is $100, or some other figure. However, the simplest method is not always the best one.

The value of the business will tend to change as time goes on. The owners hope, of course, that the change will be a positive one. Unfortunately, many business owners, once they have worked out a buy-sell agreement, forget that it contains a dynamic feature—the transaction price. As a result, a buy-sell agreement that contains a stated share value or business interest value may be woefully inadequate when a business owner dies, retires or becomes disabled. Despite the possible inadequacy of the transaction price, however, the parties to the agreement are contractually required to buy or sell at the stated price. The estate of a deceased business owner may be required to sell a business interest worth millions of dollars for only $100,000 or less if that is what the agreement calls for! Obviously, every party to the agreement has a vested interest in keeping the contractual price as current as possible.

Although the stated price is frequently used in buy-sell agreements and works just fine when it is updated as needed, another approach can be used that doesn't require that the owners remember to update the agreement. That is a formula approach, stated in the agreement, as a valuation method.

Although certainly not the only factor that can be or should be used in determining the value of a business, business earnings is the most important one. Accordingly, a formula valuation might be contained in the buy-sell agreement that determines the business value by capitalizing its earnings over a particular period at a specified interest rate. For example, the value of the business could be determined by averaging the earnings of the business for the five previous years and then dividing that amount by 8 percent or some other capitalization rate.

As an example of the formula approach, consider a buy-sell agreement that valued a business as the average earnings for the previous five-year period capitalized at 8 percent. If the business owner died in 2001 and was one of four equal partners, the value of his or her interest would be one-fourth of the value of the business. Let's calculate the value of the business using this approach, assuming the following earnings amounts.

Year	Earnings
2000	$574,000
1999	$325,000
1998	$417,000
1997	$201,000
1996	$102,000
Total	$1,619,000

Once we know the earnings for the stipulated period, we can divide it by five to determine the average. In this case, the average earnings over the five-year period amounts to $323,800 ($1,619,000 ÷ 5 = $323,800).

To capitalize the earnings at 8 percent, we only need to divide the average earnings by .08. That gives us a business value of $4,047,500 ($323,800 ÷ .08 = $4,047,500). Because the deceased business owner owned one-fourth of the business, the value of his or her business interest is $1,011,875. That amount, of course, is the buyout value.

To Maintain Insurance

An agreement to buy and sell a business interest that the buyer can't complete because of a lack of available funds has little value. To ensure that cash is available to purchase the business interest in the event of the death, disability or retirement of an owner, both life insurance and disability insurance should be maintained in an amount that is sufficient to complete the transaction. The buy-sell agreement should include a provision by virtue of which the parties commit themselves to maintaining the appropriate amount of life and disability insurance to fund the agreement.

The life insurance policy or policies may actually do double duty. The death benefit would be paid and would fund the purchase in the event of the death of the insured. However, if the insured lived to retirement, any cash values could be accessed to provide funds for a part of the purchase. For that reason, life insurance used to provide funds for a buy-sell agreement should be permanent rather than term insurance.

In a sense, the disability policy that is used to provide funds in the event of the buy-sell agreement's being triggered by the disability of an owner functions in a dual capacity. Certainly, it furnishes the cash to make the purchase of the disabled owner's business interest, either in a single sum or in periodic installments. However, it also enables the insurance company to make the difficult assessment of the business owner's disability, rather than leaving that difficult decision to the other owners. Only through the medium of insurance that provides the cash exactly at the time it is needed can an assurance that the funds will be available be given.

To Deal with the Deceased Owner's Policies

In a cross-purchase agreement, each of the owners owns and pays the premiums on policies on the lives of each of the other owners. When an owner dies, the policies he or she owned on the lives of the other owners become the property of the estate. The estate may either sell the policies to their respective insureds—the remaining owners—or surrender them for their cash value. The buy-sell agreement should indicate how these policies will be handled.

From the point of view of the estate of the deceased owner, the choice of surrender or sale of the policy or policies should make no difference. In either case, the estate will receive an amount of cash equal to the cash value. It may make a considerable difference to the other owners, however.

As individuals age, there is an increased likelihood that they will become uninsurable. By drafting the cross-purchase buy-sell agreement to give the policy insureds the option to purchase their policies from the estate, they can overcome this problem.

The uninsurable business owner will be able to add additional life insurance—the amount of life insurance carried on his or her life by the deceased business owner—without being required to qualify for it. The insured may buy an existing life insurance policy on his or her life without suffering the adverse tax consequences that would arise if it were covered under the transfer for value rule. Fortunately, the purchase of a policy by the insured is a specific exception to the transfer for value rule.

How to Handle the Sale When Insurance Proceeds Are More Than or Less Than the Price. We noted earlier that the business value can be expected to fluctuate. Because the life or disability insurance policies may be more or less than the price of the business interest, the buy-sell agreement should contain a provision that describes how that situation will be handled.

Obviously, the case in which the life insurance proceeds exceed the agreement's purchase price is considerably different from the one in which the insurance proceeds are less than the agreed-upon price.

In the first case (when the insurance proceeds exceed the agreement's purchase price), the excess insurance proceeds may be retained by the business (if the agreement is a stock redemption or entity purchase agreement) or by the remaining owner. However, some buy-sell agreements provide that the actual buyout price is the greater of the agreement price and the death benefit proceeds. This approach has the beneficial effect of providing a minimum guaranteed price for the business interest despite any value fluctuation.

In those cases where the insurance proceeds are less than the agreement price, the buy-sell agreement should detail how the deficit will be paid by the buyer. In many cases, the excess price is payable by the buyer or buyers to the heirs over a period of years at a specified rate of interest. This obligation should be evidenced by an interest-bearing note or notes issued by the remaining business owners or by the business.

It should be clear that the written and insurance-funded buy-sell agreement is vital to the orderly transfer of a business interest to the remaining owners. The form that the buy-sell agreement takes, however, can be as an agreement between the owners themselves or between each owner and the business. In other words, the buy-sell agreement may be a cross-purchase plan or an entity plan. Let's turn our attention now to how these two approaches to the buyout differ, when each is indicated and their respective advantages and disadvantages.

Forms of Buy-Sell Agreements

We will begin our examination of the two types of buy-sell agreements by looking at the entity plan. In our discussion of the entity plan (which is an agreement between a partnership and its partners), you should bear in mind that, unless it is indicated to the contrary, the factors that apply to the entity agreement also apply to the complete redemption of an owner's stock under a stock redemption agreement.

The Entity Plan. Under an *entity plan*, the parties to the buy-sell agreement are the business owner and the business. All of the buy-sell provisions that we looked at earlier apply to both of the parties.

The funding for the buyout under the entity arrangement is provided by life and disability insurance owned and paid for by the business on the life of each of its owners. Since only one life insurance policy and one disability insurance policy is required for each owner, this arrangement simplifies the administration of the insurance, especially when there are a substantial number of business owners. Another reason why an entity plan might be favored is if there were a substantial age difference between the business owners that would result in a large premium difference.

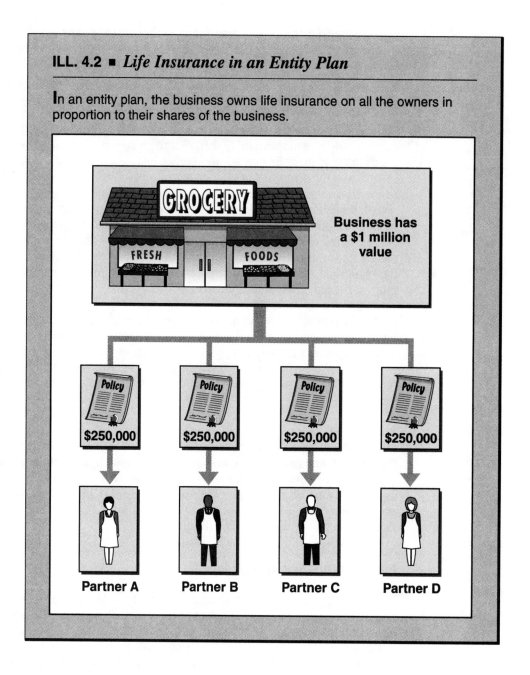

ILL. 4.2 ■ *Life Insurance in an Entity Plan*

In an entity plan, the business owns life insurance on all the owners in proportion to their shares of the business.

GROCERY

FRESH   FOODS

Business has a $1 million value

Policy $250,000   Policy $250,000   Policy $250,000   Policy $250,000

Partner A   Partner B   Partner C   Partner D

Although the life and disability insurance premiums would not be deductible regardless of whether the insurance was owned by the business or by the business owners, the benefit when received would be entirely income tax free. Let's look at a graphic representation of the insurance policy ownership under an entity plan.

As we see in Ill. 4.2, the $1,000,000 partnership owned by four partners would require funding by only four life insurance policies of $250,000 apiece.

In addition to the obvious simplicity of the entity plan, the plan has certain other advantages and disadvantages. The advantages of an entity plan include:

- The number of insurance policies required to fund the agreement is minimized. When we examine the cross-purchase plan, this advantage will become more apparent. In the entity plan, there is a need for only one insurance policy for each business owner. With the availability of universal life insurance, it is possible to maintain only a single policy per owner despite subsequent increases in the death benefit that may be required to keep up with an increasing business value.

- Premium payments are equalized. Because the premiums for all of the policies that are being used to fund the buy-sell agreement are paid for by the business, each owner pays an equal share of the premiums regardless of whether he or she is older or younger than his or her co-owners. This is in contrast to the premiums for policies used to fund a cross-purchase plan which are owned and paid for by the owners. In that case, a younger owner will usually pay more for the same coverage on an older owner than vice versa. There are, however, other methods of equalizing, or largely equalizing, the premium payments for insureds of widely differing ages.

- The policies' cash values are available to the business to help meet cash needs. Although the business could, possibly, borrow from other sources or obtain additional paid-in cash from the owners, the availability of the cash values is a simpler and, probably, quicker means of raising the needed cash.

Like most arrangements, the entity plan has certain disadvantages as well as advantages. The principal disadvantages are the following:

- The life insurance cash values are considered an asset of the business and, as such, are attachable by the business' creditors. Although the partners' joint and severable liability would also result in any policy's being subject to the creditors of the partnership, the same would not be true for corporate stockholders whose liability is limited.

- The insurance proceeds inflate the value of the business, which results in the remaining owners receiving a greater value than the deceased owner. This has, largely, been ignored in most entity plans.

- The entity plan used in a corporate setting is called a stock redemption. The redemption by the corporation of a deceased stockholder's interest does not increase the remaining stockholders' cost basis for their own interest, so that a subsequent sale of their interest will generally result in a greater income tax liability than if the buyout were made under a cross-purchase plan. (In a partnership, life insurance proceeds from any source increase the partners' basis.)

The Cross-Purchase Plan. Under a *cross-purchase plan*, the parties to the buy-sell agreement are each of the business owners. The business, itself, plays no part.

The funding for the buyout under the cross-purchase plan is provided by life insurance owned and paid for by each of the business owners on the life of the other business owners. In the simplest case—in which there are two partners or stockholders, for example—each owner would own and be the beneficiary of a life insurance policy under which the other owner was the insured.

Although the administration of the life insurance policies is easy when a business has two owners, it becomes increasingly more complicated when the number of owners increases. For example, although only two life insurance policies are required to fund a cross-purchase plan to which there are two parties, six life insurance policies are required when there are three owners, and twelve policies when there are four owners.

Because the amount of life insurance proceeds required to fund a cross-purchase plan is the same as needed to fund an entity plan, the larger number of policies generally required for the cross-purchase plan means that each policy's face amount is smaller. In addition to each policy usually carrying a policy fee, many companies charge a higher premium per thousand dollars of coverage for smaller policies. The result is higher premiums for the needed coverage under a cross-purchase plan. The simple equation for determining the number of life insurance policies needed to fund a cross-purchase plan is as follows:

$$\text{Number of policies needed} = n \times (n - 1)$$

Where "n" represents the number of owners (i.e., partners or stockholders). If there were five partners who were parties to a cross-purchase plan, the number of policies required would be:

$$5 \times (5 - 1) = 20 \text{ policies}$$

In addition to the flurry of life insurance policies that are needed as the number of partners or stockholders increases, a potential problem exists in cases where there is an age disparity between the owners.

Let's return to our simple partnership in which there are two owners, Bill and Bob. Assume that Bill is age 55 and Bob is age 30. Bill will own and pay the premiums on the policy insuring Bob. Since Bob is only 30 years old, the premium that Bill pays is quite modest, especially when compared with the premium for the policy insuring Bill, who is age 55, that Bob pays. Because Bob will be paying the premium on the policy insuring Bill while Bill pays for the policy insuring Bob, Bob could complain that he is paying a disproportionately large premium.

While it could be argued that it is appropriate for Bob to pay the higher premium because he is more likely to end up with the business (since Bill is older, he is more likely to die before Bob), the fact is that the disproportionate premium payments may be an insurmountable obstacle that stands in the way of providing a funded buy-sell agreement. To the extent that it does that, it should be abandoned in favor of the entity plan.

As we saw when we looked at the entity plan, the insurance premiums would not be deductible. However, the benefit, when received by the business owner, would be entirely income tax free. Let's look at a graphic representation of the insurance policy ownership under a cross-purchase plan. You will notice that each business owner owns a policy on the life of each other owner. In turn, each other owner owns a policy on his or her life.

ILL. 4.3 ■ *The Cross Purchase Plan Policy Ownership*

In a cross purchase plan, the owners purchase life insurance on each other. For the four-owner business illustrated below, each owner must purchase three policies — for a total of 12 policies.

We see in Ill. 4.3 that by simply adding up the arrows that point to each of the business owners (the "partners"), the death of partner A will result in the payment of three death claims: on each of the policies owned by partners B, C and D. The larger number of policy *owners* (as opposed to the number of *policies*) under the cross-purchase plan also gives rise to another concern when compared with the entity plan.

Under the entity plan, all owners must have access to the books. If the premium for a policy is not paid, all of the owners may know about it. Not so in the cross-purchase plan. Each of the policies is owned personally by the prospective purchasers on the lives of the prospective sellers. There are no guarantees to ensure that the premiums are paid when due. As a result, policies may be allowed to lapse without the knowledge of any of the other owners.

■ HOW THE TRANSACTION DIFFERS ACCORDING TO ORGANIZATION TYPE

In the previous section, we looked at the cross-purchase plan and the entity plan principally as they relate to general partnerships. Based on the knowledge that we have of each of these agreements' use in the partnership, let's expand our discussion to include the other two basic types of organization: the sole proprietorship and the corporation.

The Sole Proprietorship

By definition, a sole proprietorship has only a single owner. For most purposes, the sole proprietor and his or her business are one and the same. However, many sole proprietors are interested in transferring the business upon their death, disability or retirement. Often the reasons for this interest are the unfortunate consequences that ensue if the business is liquidated.

In Chapter 2, we discussed what happens when there is no succession. Liquidation, regardless of whether it is planned for, has the following results:

- The surviving family loses its income. In many cases, the income provided by the sole proprietorship constituted the lion's share, if not all, of the family livelihood. When the sole proprietor dies, the assets and liabilities of the business become a part of the owner's estate, and the income that was generated by the business stops. The income cessation is both immediate and abrupt.

- The business assets shrink. The business that may have been valued at $1 million the day before the owner died may be worth $200,000 the day after his or her death. That is an $800,000 loss. In addition to the shrinkage of the business assets, the death may also result in substantial expenses. Costs incurred for the business owner's last illness, funeral, estate administration, taxes and debts—both business and personal—add another substantial burden on the depleted assets.

- Employees are dislocated. The employees—some of whom may have been employed for many years—no longer have jobs.

For these and other reasons, the sole proprietor may want to transfer the business upon his or her death, disability or retirement rather than liquidate it. When family retention of the sole proprietorship isn't an option, the obvious answer may be to transfer the business to an employee. The long-term employee is often the most logical purchaser of the sole proprietorship.

The buy-sell agreement that is used to formalize the mutual understanding between the sole proprietor and the employee can't be easily categorized as an entity plan or a cross-purchase plan. It really is neither. Instead, it is a proprietorship purchase agreement.

The proprietorship purchase agreement should contain many of the same commitments and provisions that are found in any well-drafted buy-sell agreement. However, certain provisions are somewhat unique to the proprietorship purchase agreement. Let's look at the important commitments and provisions that should be contained in the agreement.

To Buy. The employee must agree to purchase the sole proprietorship business interest upon the occurrence of the triggering event, such as the death, disability or retirement of the sole proprietor.

To Sell. The sole proprietor agrees to sell his or her business interest in the event of disability or retirement and commits his or her estate to sell the business interest to the employee in the event of death.

To Restrict Sale. The sole proprietor makes a commitment that he or she will not sell the business interest during his or her lifetime without first offering it to the employee. This provision of the proprietorship purchase agreement restricting the lifetime sale of the business serves two essential functions. First, it helps to protect the employee in the event that another prospective purchaser offers the sole proprietor more for the business than was agreed upon by the employee and the sole proprietor. Second, the lifetime restriction on the sale is important if the value recited in the agreement is to be accepted by the IRS as the fair market value for estate tax purposes.

To Buy and Sell at a Particular Price. The price at which the estate or the sole proprietor must sell and the employee must buy must be stated or determinable. Although a simple statement of business value is acceptable, a formula for determining the business value that is agreed to by both the buyer and seller will tend to ensure that any fluctuation in business value will be reflected in the proprietorship purchase agreement. If the statement of dollar value is used, it is important, of course, that the business be revalued each year or when its value undergoes substantial change.

To Maintain Insurance. Although insurance is not absolutely necessary to provide the cash needed to implement a business buyout, an agreement to buy a business interest that the employee can't complete because of a lack of available funds has little value. To ensure that cash is available to purchase the business interest in the event of the death, disability or retirement of the sole proprietor, life insurance and disability insurance should be maintained in an amount that is sufficient to complete the transaction. The proprietorship purchase agreement should include a provision by virtue of which the employee commits himself or herself to maintaining the appropriate amount of life and disability insurance to fund the agreement. In addition, arrangements should be made with the insurance carrier to inform the sole proprietor in the event the premium is not paid on a timely basis. The agreement should also authorize the sole proprietor to make the premium payment on behalf of the employee and deduct it from the employee's salary.

The maintaining of life insurance by the employee on the life of the business owner, who is usually older, sometimes presents a large financial burden. Because the business owner and his or her family have an important stake in ensuring that the buyout takes place as planned (and, of course, that usually requires that insurance coverage be in force), the owner may want to finance the life insurance for the employee or use a split-dollar method of financing it.

If the owner is financing the life insurance purchase, it is advisable to have a provision in the proprietorship purchase agreement that the amount financed by the business owner will be paid to the estate out of the death benefit proceeds. The business owner's financial interest in a policy using a collateral assignment split dollar method will usually be evidenced by notes signed by the employee. Regardless of the financing method used, if any, it is only through the medium of insurance that provides the cash exactly at the time it is needed that an assurance that the funds will be available can be given.

How to Handle the Sale When Insurance Proceeds Are More Than or Less Than the Price.   Because the business value can be expected to fluctuate and because the insurance policies may be more or less than the price of the business interest, some provision should be made for it. The proprietorship purchase agreement should contain a provision that describes how the buyout will be handled if the life insurance proceeds are more or less than the value of the business.

When the insurance proceeds exceed the agreement's purchase price, the excess insurance proceeds may be kept by the employee. The proprietor purchase agreement may provide, however, that the actual buyout price will be the greater of the agreement price and the death benefit proceeds. By inserting such a provision, the family will receive a minimum guaranteed price for the business regardless of any fluctuation in the value of the business. Regardless of the approach decided upon, it should be well-communicated to all parties to the agreement and to the heirs. A failure to communicate it completely may easily lead to disagreement upon the death of the owner and, possibly, to legal action.

When the insurance proceeds are less than the agreement price, the proprietorship purchase agreement should detail how the additional funds will be paid by the employee-buyer. Often, the additional amount owed is payable by the buyer to the heirs over a period of years at a specified rate of interest. This payment arrangement should be evidenced by an interest-bearing note or notes issued by the employee.

The Role of a Trustee.   Although not essential to the operation of a proprietorship purchase agreement, a trustee is desirable. A trustee, especially if that role is filled by a corporate trustee, can add a certain objectivity to the purchase and can help to resolve any difficulty that may be anticipated in working with the heirs. The agreement should delineate the duties of the trustee and the trustee's fee.

The Employee's Assumption of Obligations.   Although the price negotiated between the business owner and the employee for the purchase of the proprietorship generally includes all of the assets and liabilities of the company, a proprietorship's obligations are the personal obligations of the proprietor. As the proprietor's personal obligations, the company's liabilities would generally become the obligation of the estate. For that reason, the proprietorship purchase agreement should clearly state that upon the death of the business owner the employee-buyer assumes the liabilities of the business.

The Corporation

Many of the issues and decisional factors that apply to transferring the business interest in the case of the partnership—and to some extent, the sole proprietorship—also apply in the corporation. The entity plan that we have examined in connection with the general partnership has a new name when it is applied to the corporate form. In the corporation, an entity plan is called a stock redemption plan. It is, of course, a redemption of the entire interest rather than the partial redemption that we briefly examined under Code Section 303. This total redemption is sometimes referred to as a Section 302 redemption.

From a legal perspective, of course, the corporation has certain fundamental differences. One of the most important differences is that the corporation has a life that is legally separate and distinct from that of its owners. As a result, unlike the partnership or sole proprietorship, the corporation does not legally end at the death of an owner. It may be liquidated by the heirs for business reasons, such as the unavailability of competent successors or the unreplaceable decedent, but that liquidation is not mandated by law.

Another important difference is that the corporation and its owners are separate tax entities. Each is liable for its own income taxes.

Let's turn our attention now to the differences in transferring the corporate interest that result from the fact that it is a corporation. We will find that the differences fall into a number of categories, including legal, financial and taxation and that these differences may preclude certain approaches and suggest others.

Legal Issues. We noted earlier that a corporation is a distinct legal entity. It is not the owner "in a different form." Legally, the stockholder and the corporation are distinct. Furthermore, the permitted activities of the corporation are generally governed by state law. One of those governed activities is the corporation's ability to redeem its own stock.

Professional corporations may have more stringent restrictions applied than commercial corporations in the matter of redeeming stock. In addition, many states permit a corporation, regardless of the type, to redeem stock only when it has sufficient surplus to effect the redemption.

In the case where state law requires surplus to redeem stock, the stock redemption agreement could contain a provision to the effect that the corporation will take those measures necessary to create the needed surplus. That can be done through a recapitalization and par value reduction or through a revaluing of the assets of the corporation. Restrictions on the corporation's ability to redeem its stock may indicate that a cross-purchase plan makes more sense in that situation. Legal issues are not the only issues that may affect the agreement choice.

Financial Issues. We saw in our examination of the sole proprietorship and the partnership that the owners were fully liable for the debts of their respective organizations. That is not the case in the corporation.

Legally, the corporate stockholder is generally liable for the debts of the corporation only to the extent of the value of his or her investment in the corporation. This limitation of liability, however, is not absolute. It does not apply to the professional liability of a stockholder or, generally, when the liability is due to the owner's fraudulent actions. In addition, owners of small corporations often must also make themselves personally liable in order for the corporation to receive needed credit.

However, when those exceptions to the rule don't apply, the assets of the stockholder are not attachable in payment of corporate debts. The application of this rule in the selection of a corporate buy-sell agreement may cause the owners to favor a cross-purchase plan. The reason for that is any life insurance owned by the corporation that may fund a stock redemption plan is subject—both as to its cash value and death benefit—to the creditors of the corporation. As a result, the deceased stockholder's estate and the remaining stockholders could find that the death benefits that were intended to purchase the stock had been attached by creditors to satisfy corporate debts.

If the buy-sell agreement were of the cross-purchase variety, the life insurance policies purchased to fund the buyout would have been purchased and owned by the stockholders rather than by the corporation. Because the personal assets of the stockholders are not generally attachable to satisfy corporate debts, the life insurance policies would be beyond the reach of the corporation's creditors.

There is an exception to the cross-purchase plan funding policies' ability to avoid attachment by corporate creditors in the case of policies purchased under a split dollar arrangement. Sometimes, especially when the corporation is in a lower income tax bracket than the stockholder and there is a substantial age difference between or among the owners, parties to a corporate cross-purchase plan may look to the corporate coffers to help pay for the life insurance policies that are used to fund the agreement's buyout. In such a case, the corporation's interest in the policies may be attachable by corporate creditors.

Administrative Issues.   Closely related to the exposure of corporate-owned life insurance to the claims of creditors is the corporation's use of the policies' cash value when the policies are used in the stock redemption plan.

In the case of life insurance owned by the corporation—as it would be when it is used to fund a stock redemption agreement—the business has unfettered access to the cash value for business purposes. Because the cash values of permanent life insurance policies may be very substantial, they may provide a welcome source of cash for expansion, inventory purchase or funding a temporary cash flow shortfall. Although the problem of creditor attachment is an important one, the corporation's desire to use cash values may, nonetheless, cause stockholders to favor a stock redemption plan.

Tax Issues.   The tax issue differences with respect to the corporate form are, perhaps, the most numerous of the concerns that militate against a particular arrangement or suggest one. The important tax issues relate to the following concerns:

- cost basis on a subsequent sale of stock by remaining stockholders;

- after-tax cost of insurance premiums; and

- attribution of relatives' stock holdings to the departing business owner.

Let's examine each of these concerns.

Stockholders who continue as business owners after the death of a stockholder may subsequently want to sell their stock shares either to co-stockholders or to outsiders. When they sell those shares, they will incur a tax liability based upon the profit that they realize. That profit, of course, is measured by the difference between the price the seller receives for the stock and its cost basis. Generally, the greater the profit realized, the greater will be the tax liability. The stockholder's cost basis is usually equal to the price he or she paid for it.

When the stockholder acquires additional shares of stock by purchasing them from the estate of a deceased stockholder—as would be the case when a cross-purchase plan was implemented—the value of his or her stake in the company increases as a result of the increased number of shares owned. Likewise, when a corporation purchases and retires a deceased stockholder's stock from his or her estate under a stock redemption agreement, the value of the remaining stockholders' stake also increases. The stake increases because the value of each of the shares has increased with the redemption and retirement of the deceased's interest. Although there may be some minor difference in the resulting value of the remaining stockholder's stake, the value will be approximately the same. What will not be the same is the cost basis of those stakes.

In the first case (the cross-purchase plan), the stockholder's cost basis will be increased by the purchase price of the stocks—even though those stocks were purchased by funds received tax free from the life insurance policy. As a result of the cross-purchase plan, the remaining stockholder's cost basis in the firm's stocks will be a combination of his or her investment in the company *plus* the cash paid for the deceased stockholder's stocks. If the deceased stockholder's interest was purchased by the corporation, the stockholder would have received no increase in cost basis. Let's look at what that means on a subsequent sale.

For an example of the difference in result on a subsequent sale, assume that Bob Bigbucks paid $100,000 for his one-third share in Bigbucks Manufacturing, Inc. That one-third interest is worth $500,000 at the time his co-stockholder, Bill Olderman, dies. Because the buy-sell agreement provided that the surviving stockholders would own the company equally upon the death of a stockholder, Bob and his remaining co-stockholder each own a one-half interest in a corporation worth $1.5 million. If Bob were to sell his one-half interest, he would realize $750,000.

If the buy-sell agreement were a cross-purchase plan, Bob's cost basis on that subsequent sale would be the total of his investment of $100,000 and the cost of his subsequent buyout of his deceased co-stockholder of $250,000. In other words, Bob's total cost basis would be $350,000. Upon the sale, Bob would realize a taxable profit amounting to $400,000 ($750,000 – $350,000 = $400,000). If Bob paid a 20 percent capital gains tax on the profit, his tax would amount to $80,000.

If the buy-sell agreement were a stock redemption, the numbers would be different. Bob's cost basis on the subsequent sale would be his total investment of $100,000. Because the corporation, rather than Bob, purchased the deceased stockholder's shares, Bob's cost basis isn't increased even though his stock value was. Upon the sale of his business interest for the same $750,000, because Bob's cost basis is only $100,000, he would realize a taxable profit amounting to $650,000 ($750,000 – $100,000 = $650,000).

If Bob paid a 20 percent capital gains tax on the profit, his tax would amount to $130,000. The use of a stock redemption plan cost Bob an additional $50,000 in taxes.

The after-tax cost of insurance premiums may also cause stockholders to choose one form of corporate buy-sell agreement rather than another. The general guideline for deciding on which of two entities should pay for anything relates to the tax deductibility of the purchase and the relative tax rates of the entities. As a general statement, it is more cost-effective to pay for something that is tax deductible in the highest tax bracket. Conversely, it is more cost-effective to pay for something that is not tax deductible in the entity with the lowest tax bracket. Because the corporation and its stockholders are separate and distinct tax entities, each of whom may own life insurance designed to provide funding for a stock purchase, this type of analysis may be important.

Consider the after-tax cost of paying $1 on a non-deductible basis in a 36 percent tax bracket. In order to have $1 after taxes, the entity would need to earn $1.56. The $.56 would be paid in income taxes, leaving $1 for purposes of making the purchase ($1.56 × .36 = $.56). On the other hand, if the entity was in only a 15 percent tax bracket, it would need only $1.18 to produce the same after-tax $1 ($1.18 × .15 = $.18).

While the results aren't startling when only $1 is involved, what if the total is $50,000 in annual premium? If the corporation is in a 15 percent tax bracket, it needs to earn only $58,824 to have the $50,000 to pay the premium. If stockholders, each of whom are in a 36 percent tax bracket, are to pay the premium to fund a cross-purchase plan, they would need to earn $78,125 jointly to produce $50,000 to pay the life insurance premiums. The difference in approaches may cost the individuals almost $20,000 each year in additional tax costs.

This additional cost may cause stockholders to avoid a cross-purchase plan, even though it would have enabled them to increase their cost basis on a subsequent sale or gift of the stocks. (It needn't be stated, of course, that the cost basis problem is overcome if the stock transfer is made upon the stockholder's death because of the step-up.)

The marginal income tax rates for individuals and for corporations are shown below:

Joint Individual Tax Rates		Corporate Tax Rates*	
$0 – $42,349	15%	$0 – $50,000	15%
$42,350 – $102,299	28%	$50,001 – $75,000	25%
$102,300 – $155,949	31%	$75,001 – $100,000	34%
$155,950 – $278,449	36%	$100,001 – $335,000	39%
$278,450 and over	39.6%	$335,001 – $10,000,000	34%
		$10,000,001 – $15,000,000	35%
		$15,000,001 – $18,333,332	38%
		$18,333,333 and over	35%

* Personal service corporations are taxed at a flat rate of 35%.

The final tax concern that we will address in this section is one called *attribution*. The attribution concept is a fairly simple one, and it applies only to a stock redemption; it does not apply to a stock purchase incident to a cross-purchase plan.

Specifically, all of the stock shares owned by certain family members in a family business are deemed to be owned by each of the family members. The ownership of stock owned by the stockholder's spouse, children, grandchildren and parents is attributed to the stockholder when the stockholder or his or her estate redeems stock. That is important in the case of a stock redemption agreement because unredeemed stock attributable to a deceased stockholder will result in the redemption being considered an income-taxable dividend instead of a non-income taxable stock redemption.

However, if a total redemption is effected and, subsequently, determined to be in violation of the attribution rules, there may be a partial remedy that can keep the entire distribution from being considered a dividend. If the estate fails to qualify for a Section 302 stock redemption (because of the attribution problem) but qualifies for a Section 303 stock redemption, only the redemption in excess of the applicable Section 303 amount would be considered a dividend. Although this remedy would probably not solve the estate's problem completely, it may help. When several family stockholders are in the corporation, it may make much more sense to use a cross-purchase plan instead of a stock redemption in order to avoid the attribution issue.

No buy-sell approach exists that will be the most favorable in every situation. Accordingly, it is important to work with the client and his or her attorney and accountant to consider the issues that apply to each type of buy-sell agreement and the specific characteristics of the business in order to determine which approach will work best in each situation. (Consult Dearborn's *Business Insurance* for a comprehensive look at the decisional factors in plan selection.)

▪ REPLACING THE KEY PERSON— PRACTICAL NEEDS OF THE BUSINESS

The loss of a key person through death, disability or retirement is often a devastating blow to the business. Whether the business is organized as a sole proprietorship, a partnership or a corporation makes little difference. If the business is to succeed, a departed key person must be replaced.

In Chapter 1, we examined the effects on an organization of a key person's loss. We noted that the key person's loss can affect the ability of a business to:

- meet its sales or production goals;

- negotiate appropriate credit; or

- succeed generally.

If the individual is, in fact, a key person, the business has little choice but to replace him or her. Because finding a key person is expensive and, often, a relatively long process, a need exists to provide funds to ensure that the business can handle the expense and profit loss during the search period.

When the key person has departed through retirement, the need to replace him or her would normally have been recognized well before the retirement and a replacement hired while the key person was still employed. It is when the key person's replacement is required because of his or her death or disability that businesses experience many of their problems.

When the business has acknowledged that the loss of a key person through death or disability is a risk that should be insured against, the important task is to determine how much insurance will adequately compensate the business for its economic loss. Once the amount needed to compensate the business is determined, it's a simple task to purchase the appropriate amount of life insurance and disability insurance. Although life insurance is the coverage most frequently purchased, the disabled key person may be as lost to the business as the deceased key person. For that reason, key person disability should not be overlooked. The business should be the beneficiary, and the insurance should be owned and paid for by the business.

Let's look at some of the approaches taken to determine the extent of the economic loss that would be sustained by the business as a result of the loss of a key person. The appropriate amount of key person insurance that a company should have on its key individuals is a combination of the value of the economic loss plus the cost to locate and hire a suitable replacement.

The Present Value of the Projected Loss of Earnings

Under this method of determining the economic loss to the business, the earnings that are anticipated for the future are estimated. The earnings that would be anticipated for the future *without* the key person are then estimated. The present value, using a conservative rate of interest, of the difference in the two earnings streams is determined. This is an estimation of the economic loss to the business of the loss of the key person.

The Excess Salary Test

Using the excess salary method to estimate the economic loss to a business upon the loss of a key person, the salary that would have to be paid to an employee hired to accomplish the *routine* tasks done by the key person is determined. This amount is then subtracted from the actual salary paid to the key person. The difference between the two salaries—sometimes called the "excess" salary—is deemed to be the cost of the individual's performing the "key" duties. This excess salary is multiplied by the number of years that it would take to locate and train a replacement.

Under this approach, if the key person is receiving an income of $100,000, and someone could be hired to accomplish his or her routine duties for $45,000, the excess salary would be $55,000. If the business anticipates that it would require two years to find a suitable replacement and train him or her, the economic loss would be $110,000 ($55,000 × 2 = $110,000).

When the key person is an owner and this approach is used, an additional complication is added. That complication relates to the fact that an owner customarily can attribute a part of his or her salary to a return on the investment made in the business.

One Year's Profit

Under this approach, no economic loss is determined. Instead, the use of one year's business profit as assumed loss permits the business to spend one year in finding and training the key person's replacement.

Contribution to Earnings

Under this approach, the value of the contribution made by the key person to the earnings of the business are estimated. To make the calculation, you must know either the average book value or the stockholder's equity for the last five years. In addition, you must know the average business net income before taxes for the same five-year period.

The steps in this approach are as follows:

1. Multiply the average book value of the assets by a fair percentage return that could have been received if the funds had been invested elsewhere; this is the hypothetical return on assets.

2. Subtract the hypothetical return on assets from the average business net income for the five-year period; the result is the income that is attributable to management's expertise.

3. Multiply the income that is attributable to management by the number of years it would take to find and train new management.

These four approaches to valuing a key person are, at best, estimations. Regardless of the method used to estimate the value of a key person, it is important to add to that number the cost to locate and train the individual's replacement. Finally, the life insurance and disability insurance should be purchased.

Measuring the insurable value of a key person has traditionally been based on the amount of the key person's compensation multiplied by a factor that accounts for the loss to the business and the cost to replace the individual. However, that is not the only criterion that may be legitimately employed. The value of a key person may be based on:

- the individual's specialized skills or knowledge;

- the key person's relationship with lenders and investors that may have given the corporation access to capital; and

- the imputed value of patents held by the key person.

The biggest problem in estimating the value of a key person is that the factors that are used are subjective and difficult to quantify. As a guide, however, many insurers consider five to ten years of salary as reasonable key person indemnification.

■ TAX AND ESTATE PLANNING ISSUES

The tax and estate planning issues that may arise in any individual case depend, of course, on the specific circumstances that surround it. However, certain general observations can be made.

If the transfer of the business interest is effected as a result of the disability or retirement of the business owner, some income tax issues may arise. The severity of the income tax issues depend upon the profit realized upon the sale. If the business interest transfer is the result of the owner's death, the estate will not face income tax concerns with respect to the sale because of a stepped-up basis that it receives upon the owner's death. Instead, it will face estate tax issues.

The estate tax concerns are generally twofold. The first concern is that the IRS will accept the buy-sell agreement valuation for estate tax purposes. The standard for value is set forth in Treasury Regulation 20.2031-1(b) which states that:

> *The price at which the property would change hands between a willing buyer and a willing seller, neither being under any compulsion to buy and sell and both having reasonable knowledge of relevant facts.*

Because special factors exist in the case of a buy-sell agreement between family members, successfully facing a challenge by the IRS will require that the agreement:

- be a bona fide business agreement;

- not be a device to transfer the business to family members for less than full and adequate consideration; and

- have terms comparable to similar arrangements entered into between persons in an arms-length agreement.

The other estate tax issue concerns the payment of any estate taxes due. The generally preferred method of providing for the payment of estate tax liabilities is through the use of life insurance purchased and owned by an irrevocable life insurance trust. A similar trust may be established for the purpose of buying life insurance that will be used to replace any family income that cannot be replaced by the investment of the business interest sale proceeds.

■ CASE STUDY: BIGBUCKS MANUFACTURING

Two years ago, at age 60, Bill Bigbucks had anticipated that, upon his death or retirement as president of Bigbucks Manufacturing, the business would be liquidated. No heir was interested in taking over the business, the business had no other owners, and the costs to update the technology were too substantial. As a result, Bill's will had been changed to give the executor the needed powers to maximize the liquidated value, and an irrevocable life insurance trust had been established which owns a life insurance policy on Bill's life in the amount of $1,030,357.

In the intervening two years, a number of changes had occurred. Bill hired an executive from a competitor who bought a 40 percent stake in the company and became

Bill's partner in Bigbucks Manufacturing. Bob Wilson is a 45-year-old engineer who ran the competitor's manufacturing operation. Since joining Bigbucks Manufacturing, Bob has managed to make significant technological advances in the way Bigbucks operates. As a result, the company's competitive position has improved substantially. Bob has told Bill that he is interested in buying out Bill's business interest when he retires or dies.

Bill looked at the company's balance sheet to see what such a change in plans would mean. The balance sheet showed the following financial information:

	Current Value
Equipment	$750,000
Inventory	$150,000
Accounts receivable	$200,000
Other assets	$50,000
Total balance sheet asset	$1,150,000
Patents	$1,000,000
Total assets	$2,150,000

Bill looked at his personal balance sheet. That looked as follows:

Assets		Liabilities	
Home	$575,000	Home mortgage	$225,000
Personal property	$75,000	Burial and final expenses	$10,000
Securities	$150,000	Estate administration	$50,000
IRA	$200,000	Policy loan	$25,000
Life insurance	$85,000	Other debts	$12,500
Interest sold to Bob	$860,000	Inheritance tax	$20,000
Value of the business	$1,290,000		
Total	$3,235,000		$342,500

Because the estate would be using the unlimited marital deduction for the bulk of the assets, no federal estate taxes would come due at Bill's death. At Bill's wife Beth's subsequent death, the federal estate taxes are estimated to be $264,875.

Bill's Concerns

The concerns that Bill and his partner Bob have are twofold: buying the business interest in the event of either partner's death and ensuring the survival of the business. Bill's concern about providing Beth a $150,000 annual income at his death will be resolved by the purchase of Bill's business interest at death.

The Solution

Bill and Bob enter into a buy-sell agreement that uses an entity plan approach. They chose this method instead of a cross-purchase plan to equalize the cost of the life insurance, despite the fact that Bill is 17 years older than Bob. Furthermore, because Bigbucks Manufacturing is now a partnership, the life insurance payable to the company will increase each partner's cost basis. Under the buy-sell agreement, the company agrees to purchase the deceased partner's interest at his death or retirement. Two life insurance policies are purchased to fund the agreement: $1,290,000 on Bill's life and $860,000 on Bob's life.

An additional life insurance purchase of $1 million will be made by the business to replace the economic loss to the business in the event of Bill's death before retirement. In addition, at Bill's retirement the policy's cash value can be used as a down payment on the buyout by the company of Bill's business interest. An additional $1 million life insurance policy is purchased on Bob's life for key person insurance.

The life insurance policy that was initially purchased by the irrevocable life insurance trust can be reduced from its current $1,030,357 to $264,875. That is the approximate amount of federal estate tax payable upon Beth's death.

■ SUMMARY

In this chapter we examined the factors that favor transfer of the family business rather than its retention. The principal factors that favor transfer are the decedent's minority business interest, the lack of heirs available to assume the business interest and the availability of a buyer for the interest.

The methods available to effectively transfer the business interest were discussed. In addition, the differences in those methods that result from the different types of organizations were examined.

The practical needs of the business to replace the key person were addressed. Various formulas were examined that estimate the economic need of the business upon the loss of a key person.

The tax and estate planning issues that may be consequences of the transfer of the business interest were discussed. They include the minimizing of gain on the sale, establishing the value of the business interest for estate tax purposes and replacing any family income not replaced by the sale price for the interest.

■ CHAPTER 4 QUESTIONS FOR REVIEW

1. Which of the following would NOT be a factor favoring the sale of the family business interest?

    A. Decedent's interest being a minority interest

    B. Availability of successor management in the family

    C. No heirs being available to take over the business interest

    D. Availability of a buyer for the interest

2. How many life insurance policies would be needed to fully fund a cross-purchase plan with life insurance if the plan included five partners?

    A. 5

    B. 10

    C. 20

    D. 25

3. An entity plan buy-sell agreement in a corporation is commonly referred to as what kind of plan?

    A. Stock redemption

    B. Non-qualified

    C. Cross-purchase

    D. Family attribution

4. Which of the following would NOT generally be the result of business liquidation?

    A. Surviving family members lose their income.

    B. Value of the business is reduced.

    C. Employees are dislocated.

    D. Accounts receivable are usually paid in full.

5. What is the benefit of a trustee in administering a proprietorship purchase agreement?

    A. To value the business

    B. To add objectivity to the transaction

    C. To enable the estate to obtain the highest price for the business interest

    D. To keep the business sale proceeds out of the hands of the IRS

5

Succession at Retirement

he business owner's succession at retirement allows the business something important that succession at death or disability does not. That important something is time. Instead of being faced with a management crisis precipitated by the business owner's departure due to his or her death or disability, the business has had many years to prepare for the business owner's retirement. Unfortunately, nearly one-third of chief executives within five years of retirement had not chosen a successor.

This chapter addresses the needs that both the business and the business owner have when the business owner retires. It also outlines strategies that can be implemented to make the transaction easier for both. In this chapter we will be examining certain strategies—such as private annuities and self-completing installment notes—whose applicability, documentation and implementation in any particular situation demand that the client seek competent accounting and legal counsel.

Chapter Objectives

In this chapter, you will learn:

- the needs of the business owner and the business when management succession is the result of the business owner's retirement;

- the strategies that can be implemented to meet the business and its owner's needs at retirement;

- the use of life insurance in the plan for the business owner's retirement;

- the tax and estate planning issues that must be considered by the retiring business owner; and

- the role of qualified and non-qualified retirement plans in the owner's retirement.

■■■■■

■ MANAGEMENT SUCCESSION AT THE OWNER'S RETIREMENT

Issues in Succession at Retirement

The principal considerations as the business owner reaches retirement are those that relate to making that transition as smooth as possible with minimal negative change in the business owner's lifestyle or the operation of the business. In other words, the business owner has certain requirements that must be met to satisfy his or her lifestyle needs, and the business has requirements to be met to give it the best chance to survive the transition and be profitable. Let's look at the needs of both of these entities to ensure, insofar as possible, that the change is positive.

Needs of the Retiring Business Owner

The primary needs of the business owner at retirement are not too dissimilar to those needs of anyone faced with losing their job. They are financial. In the case of the successful business owner, however, the need to replace income, although generally considered most important, is accompanied by some important tax needs. We will consider the income needs first.

Income During Retirement.   Studies have suggested that retirees need a replacement income in retirement that ranges from 50 percent to 70 percent of their pre-retirement income. Commuting costs, the need to be attired for the office and so on are not generally issues for the retiree as they are for the employee. In addition, those same studies have indicated that a higher replacement level is needed for the lower-paid employee than the higher-paid employee because fixed costs are more of a factor at the lower income levels.

These studies would seem to imply that your business owner client who is currently earning $300,000 a year should have a retirement income of something in the neighborhood of $150,000 a year. That couldn't be further from the truth. For the successful business owner who wants to continue to enjoy his or her current lifestyle during retirement, a retirement income-replacement level needs to be considerably closer to 100 percent! (If there is any doubt of the validity of this wisdom, ask yourself whether you would be willing to leave your job and forgo half your income effective tomorrow.)

A luxury once enjoyed becomes a necessity. People can live in a modest studio apartment in retirement and drive a subcompact car. But is that what the business owner wants? The successful business owner, in addition to wanting to continue doing what he or she has been doing—enjoying the country club, the golf course and the home at the lake—may want to travel and become involved in other activities that will increase the need for income rather than decrease it.

Furthermore, many of the expenses that employees normally incur during their working life for automobiles, lunches, etc. may have been business-provided perks for the business owner. He or she may never have paid for them; the business did. The point that needs to be made is that the successful business owner's needs in retirement may be considerably higher than those who were not business owners or were not as successful. It is not only income during retirement, however, that is often a concern to the business owner. Tax issues often take an important second place in the retired business owner's priorities.

Taxes. For many business owners approaching retirement, potential tax bills may be quite significant. The events that bring taxes to the forefront for the business owner are the sale of the business interest and the eventual transfer of the business owner's assets to his or her heirs.

Many businesses owe their success primarily to the drive and creativity of their owners rather than to the extent of the financial investment in the business. Although the business may have required a substantial initial investment to get it launched that initial investment may have been fully depreciated, leaving little cost basis to offset the sale price. As a result, selling the business may subject the owners to a large income tax liability. When the business owner is selling his or her stake in a family-owned corporation, there may be additional tax concerns caused by the attribution rules.

In addition, successful business owners are disproportionately represented among those individuals with estate tax problems. Those problems are frequently caused by the significant value of the business and the fact that the business may be the largest asset owned by the business owner—often by a substantial margin—with little, if any, liquidity. Poor liquidity is often the most serious problem faced by the business owner's estate. Because of that set of circumstances, estate taxes may be large, and the estate may not be in a position to pay them. This problem can affect the business itself.

Needs of the Business

The needs of and challenges faced by the business depend, in part, on the intended disposition of the business interest. If the business is to remain in the family, one of the most important concerns is ensuring that the business will not need to be sold to satisfy the estate's tax liability.

Whether the business is to remain in the business owner's family or be transferred to other owners, other needs must be addressed. We examined some of these needs in earlier chapters:

- the need to locate, hire and develop competent successor management;

- the need to replace a key person; and

- the need for sufficient cash to:

  - offset the almost inevitable economic loss suffered by the business on the loss of the key person;

  - bolster the company's financial picture for suppliers and customers; and

  - provide for the cost to replace the key person.

Locating, hiring and developing competent successor management is not typically a problem when the business is to be transferred to existing owners. In that case, since the partners or co-stockholders have been a part of the business during the tenure of the retiring business owner they have had an opportunity to gain additional management experience. However, when the business is to be retained in the family and the retiring business owner held both a majority interest and the senior management position in the firm, finding a suitable successor can be critical to the company's survival.

Regardless of whether a need to find successor management exists, the need to replace the key person normally remains. While the issue of successor management may be resolved, someone must assume the other important duties handled by the business owner. These duties may involve customer contact, maintaining supplier or banking relationships or other key functions.

Business Transition Strategies

Just as the business and the business owner face different challenges, different strategies can be implemented to meet those challenges. We have enumerated some of the more important challenges that face the business and business owner, so let's examine the strategies and techniques that can be implemented.

Strategies for the Business Owner When the Business Is Retained

Not unexpectedly, the strategies that may be most appropriate for the retiring business owner will depend upon whether the business is to be retained in the family or transferred to other owners or employees at retirement.

The business owner's needs, as we have discussed, generally fall into two categories: providing income and minimizing taxes. In those situations in which the business is to be retained in the family—and the transition includes an intrafamily transfer— two strategies suggest a means of meeting both of the business owner's needs. Those strategies are:

1. the private annuity; and

2. the self-canceling installment note.

Private Annuities in General.   Business owners are usually familiar with the basic concept of an annuity. In the case of a commercial annuity, an insurance company agrees to make fixed periodic payments to an annuitant for the remainder of his or her life in return for the payment of an annuity consideration. The annuity consideration and the amount of the periodic payments are based on the annuitant's life expectancy. Private annuities are similar in concept to a commercial annuity. The principal differences are the parties to the transaction and the nature of the consideration.

A private annuity, instead of being an agreement between an annuitant and an insurance company, is usually an agreement between the annuitant and a member of his or her family. The consideration in a private annuity, instead of being a cash payment, is often appreciated property. In the typical situation involving a private annuity, a retiring business owner sells his or her business to a family member in return for the family member's unsecured promise to make fixed periodic payments to the seller for the remainder of his or her life. Payments end at the death of the annuitant. The payments made to the seller are usually funded, at least in part, by the income generated by the transferred business.

The private annuity is generally suitable only in those situations in which a close trust relationship exists between the parties, because the annuity payments cannot be secured without adverse tax consequences. (The problem, from a tax perspective, is that the law requires recognition of the entire gain in the year of sale when the promised payments are secured.) Although that relationship may exist between partners or co-stockholders, it is more likely to exist between family members.

Although the concept of a private annuity is a simple one that requires little additional explanation, the advantages and disadvantages of the private annuity deserve a more complete examination.

Advantages of a Private Annuity. The advantages of a private annuity fall into two categories:

1. securing adequate retirement income; and

2. minimizing certain taxes while eliminating others.

Because the private annuity continues for the annuitant's life, it is an income that he or she cannot outlive. Additionally, providing retirement income using a private annuity offers certain tax advantages that would not be available using other income options. For example, a retiring business owner could obtain a retirement income by being paid a consultation fee and transferring his or her business interest at death. Alternatively, the retiring business owner could increase his or her distributive share of business profits or the stock dividends payable.

These alternative options may be unattractive from both an income tax and estate tax viewpoint. From an estate tax perspective, these alternatives may be inappropriate because the business (and, of course, any appreciation) will be included in the business owner's federal gross estate. As for income tax issues, if the income is dividend income received from a regular corporation, it is taxed on both the corporate and individual levels. If the consultation fees are paid from a regular corporation, they may be challenged by the IRS as unreasonable compensation. If they are successfully challenged, the corporation would lose its tax deduction for their payment. Even if the payments are allowed, they would be fully income taxable.

The tax advantages of a private annuity include:

- *Estate tax advantages.* The appreciating business is removed from the business owner's federal gross estate because it constitutes a bona fide sale for full and adequate compensation. Also, no part of the private annuity contract is includible in the annuitant's federal gross estate because the right to the annuity payments is extinguished upon the annuitant's death.

- *Gift tax advantages.* No gift tax liability exists because the transaction (if properly done) constitutes a sale of the interest in exchange for a full and adequate consideration.

- *Income tax advantages.* Income taxes payable upon the sale are spread out, and a part of each annuity payment is treated as a tax-free return of capital, part as capital gain and the remaining part as ordinary income. Also, no income recognition of any deferred gain occurs when the annuity terminates upon the annuitant's death. (This is a unique advantage of a private annuity.)

Disadvantages of a Private Annuity.   No strategy exists that is entirely without disadvantages. That applies to the private annuity as well. The disadvantages of a private annuity include:

- *Risk.* The business purchaser's promise to make fixed periodic annuity payments for life must be unsecured for the annuitant to avoid adverse income tax consequences. Although the avoidance of an immediate recognition of gain is certainly a goal to be sought after, the business owner may find that the inherent lack of security in an unsecured promise constitutes a greater risk than he or she is willing to take, even for a close family member.

- *Income taxes.* Because the gain on the sale of the business is crystallized upon entering into the private annuity transaction, the aggregate income taxes incurred may exceed the estate taxes saved by the removal of the business from the business owner's federal gross estate, especially if the annuitant lives substantially beyond his or her life expectancy.

- *No interest deduction.* Unlike the interest payable under an installment note, no part of a private annuity payment is treated as interest. Instead, the total payment made by the business purchaser is considered a part of the purchase price for the business (i.e., a capital expenditure). As a result, the business purchaser receives no interest deduction for any interest—even for the portion of the annuity payment that represents ordinary annuity income to the annuitant.

- *Valuation difficulty.* The amount of the annuity payment is a function of the business owner's life expectancy and the value of the business that is transferred. If the business interest being transferred is in a public corporation, there is little difficulty in valuing it. In contrast, the closely held business interest presents serious difficulties in valuation. In most situations in which a business interest is transferred for a private annuity, the business is a closely held one. As a result of this inherent difficulty in valuation, the business owner may find it difficult to convince the IRS that equal values were exchanged upon the transfer.

- *Limited cost basis.* The business purchaser in a private annuity transaction will receive an initial basis in the business equal to the present value of the prospective payments under the annuity contract. Upon the annuitant's death, the buyer's cost basis becomes the total of the actual payments made to the annuitant. Should the annuitant die immediately after receiving only one payment, the total of that one payment alone becomes the business buyer's basis. (If the business had been transferred at death, however, the buyer would have received a step-up in basis to the value at the date of death.)

- *Inflexibility.* The financial burden assumed by the business buyer, or the buyer's estate if he or she should predecease the annuitant, may prove overwhelming, especially because limiting the annuity payments to the income generated by the business would expose the transaction to a possible recharacterization as a transfer with a retained life interest. Such a recharacterization would be accompanied by adverse estate, gift or income tax consequences.

- *Diminished estate tax advantages.* The estate tax advantages that result from removing the appreciating business from the business owner's federal gross estate will be diminished if the annuitant does not expend the cash received in the annuity payment. To the extent that the payments are permitted to accumulate, they will be included in his or her federal gross estate.

Self-Canceling Installment Note. The *self-canceling installment note (SCIN)* can be seen as a hybrid of both installment note characteristics and private annuity characteristics. Although the SCIN is an installment note and is treated as such under the law, payments cease upon the death of the former business owner, just as they would under a private annuity. The advantages of a SCIN include:

- *Estate tax advantages.* The transferred business and its appreciation are removed from the business seller's federal gross estate, as they are in a private annuity, provided it is a bona fide sale. To be treated as a bona fide sale without an element of gift, the consideration to be received by the business seller should reflect both the fair market value of the business and a risk premium that compensates the seller for the risk that he or she may die before all of the installment payments have been made.

- *Estate tax advantages.* Similar to a private annuity (and unlike a traditional installment note) the unpaid balance of the installment note automatically canceled by the business seller's death is not includible in the business seller's federal gross estate.

- *Minimized risk.* Unlike the situation in a private annuity, wherein the securing of the payments causes adverse income tax consequences, the SCIN can be secured to the same extent that any other installment obligation can be secured. The securing of the SCIN does not cause the business seller to lose the ratable reporting of income from the sale.

- *Income tax advantages.* Under an installment note, including a SCIN, interest payments may be deductible by the business purchaser, thereby reducing his or her ultimate cost for the business.

- *Maximum price payable.* The business purchaser in a SCIN transaction knows the maximum amount that he or she will be required to pay for the business interest because payments terminate after a definite term if they are not terminated earlier by the death of the business seller. In the case of a private annuity transaction, the business buyer does not know the ultimate price to be paid for the business interest until the death of the business seller.

The disadvantages in using the self-canceling installment note in the purchase of a business interest are principally two:

- *Higher installment obligation.* The SCIN term of payments must be shorter than the business seller's life expectancy. If the term exceeds the business seller's life expectancy, the SCIN will be considered a private annuity. Because the term of payments must necessarily be shorter than the business seller's life expectancy, the payment must be greater than under a private annuity. In addition, the requirement that the payment include a risk premium will also increase the installment obligation.

- *May outlive the income*. For many business owners concerned about retirement income, the SCIN's definite term may be a problem. The definite term of payments may mean that payments will terminate before the business seller's death.

Whether the private annuity or self-canceling installment note is the appropriate technique in the intrafamily sale of any business depends upon the particular facts. Either approach may work well in a given situation, and both have certain drawbacks. In either case, life insurance is often owned by the corporation or by other stockholders designed to fund a buy-sell agreement at death or to provide key person coverage that may no longer be needed once the business owner retires. The cash value of that life insurance can provide a down payment for the retiring business owner's interest. Because the business owner may have continuing death benefit needs, he or she should determine whether the policies should be surrendered (and a cash payment made to the owner) or transferred.

An additional concern arises when the business owner is transferring a corporate family-owned business. That concern is known as *attribution*. Let's state the general problem and then look at what can be done about it.

The owners of many, perhaps most, family-owned regular corporations generally try to take funds from the corporation in the form of compensation. The reason for that has to do with taxation. When compensation is received, the recipient must declare it as personal income for tax purposes. However, the corporation is permitted to deduct the compensation payment that it made as a regular business expense. In a sense, it is something of a "wash." That tax treatment, however, is not extended to funds that are distributed by the corporation as dividends.

When the owners of a regular corporation receive funds from the corporation that are considered to be dividends, they must declare those dividends as personal income for tax purposes. So far, the tax issue is identical to that involving compensation. The difference is a result of the corporation's ability to deduct the payment from its income for corporate tax purposes. As we saw, the corporation may deduct the payment when it is compensation. When the payment is a dividend, however, that tax deduction is lost to the corporation. The result is that the funds are taxed in the corporation's tax bracket and in the individual stockholder's tax bracket. In other words, the funds are taxed twice—hardly a prescription for the efficient use of money.

That is the general background concerning the taxability of stock dividends and why they are often avoided in the family-owned corporation. The redemption of stock surfaces a similar problem.

A complete stock redemption under Code Section 302 calls for the corporation to acquire its stock from the stockholder in exchange for cash or other property. For the redemption to be considered an exchange, all of the stock must be redeemed. If all of the stock is not redeemed, the transaction between the stockholder and the corporation may be deemed to be the distribution of a dividend. As we have noted, when stock dividends are distributed, they are taxable income to the recipient and not deductible to the corporation.

Unlike the income tax treatment given to dividends, a stock redemption allows the stockholder to deduct his or her cost basis. If the stock redemption were for $1 mil-

---

> ## ILL. 5.1 ■ *Less Than Complete Stock Redemptions*
>
> It is easy to see how the IRS might reasonably consider a less-than-complete redemption to be a dividend by envisioning the case in which the stockholder owns all of the outstanding stock.
>
> If he or she were to redeem half of the stock and retire it as treasury stock, the sole stockholder would still own all of the outstanding stock. The stockholder's ownership stake would not have changed, but he or she would have been able to deduct the stock's basis from the distribution rather than declare all of it as taxable income.

lion and the stockholder had a $400,000 cost basis, only $600,000 would be taxable and would, possibly, qualify for favorable long-term capital gains rates. If the redemption were considered a dividend, the entire $1 million would be considered taxable income and subject to the ordinary income tax rates, which are usually higher. The amount at stake in ensuring that the transaction is considered an exchange can be enormous.

But if all of the stockholder's shares are redeemed by the corporation, doesn't that automatically qualify as a total stock redemption and avoid the problem of being considered a dividend? The answer is, unfortunately, no. Stock that is owned by certain members of the redeeming stockholder's family is deemed to be owned by the stockholder. In other words, its ownership is attributed to the redeeming stockholder. That is the fundamental family attribution problem that is encountered in family-owned corporations. The problem of family attribution is a very real and potentially costly one.

Under the family attribution rules, a shareholder is deemed to own stock that is owned, directly or indirectly, by or for his or her:

- spouse

- children

- grandchildren

- parents

A way to remember whose stock ownership is covered by the family attribution rules is to remember that it is "one up, one to the side and two down" which refers to parents, spouse, children and grandchildren, respectively.

The net effect of the family attribution rules is to cause the ownership of family-owned company stock by any one of those listed family members to result in the redemption by the business owner to be considered a dividend. There is, however, a way to deal with this problem. It's called a waiver of family attribution rules.

Here is an example of family attribution. If Bill Jones owns 500 shares of stock in the family-owned Jones Manufacturing Co., Inc., and his daughter Sarah owns 200 shares, Bill would be deemed to own all 700 shares for purposes of the family attribution rules.

To qualify for a waiver of the family attribution rules in the case of the complete redemption of the business owner's stake in the family-owned corporation, the IRS demands that several requirements be met. However, if the requirements are met, the stock redemption will be treated as an exchange rather than a dividend distribution. Those requirements include the following:

- *Ten-Year Look-Forward Rule.* Under the 10-year look-forward rule, the total stock redemption will be considered an exchange rather than a dividend, despite the family stock ownership, if—immediately after the redemption—the shareholder has no interest in the corporation and doesn't acquire any within ten years from the redemption date (other than by bequest or inheritance).

- *Ten-Year Look-Back Rule.* Under the 10-year look-back rule, the waiver of family attribution isn't available if either of the following two limitations applies:

  1. Any portion of the redeemed stock was acquired within the prior 10-year period from a person whose stock would be attributable to the redeemed stockholder; or

  2. A person owns stock at the time of the redemption that is attributable to the redeemed stockholder and the person acquired stock in the redeeming corporation from the redeemed stockholder within the 10-year period prior to the redemption unless the stock is redeemed in the same transaction.

If the limitations in the 10-year look-back rule don't apply and the business owner files an agreement in which he or she agrees to notify the IRS of the acquisition of any prohibited interest in the corporation within the 10-year period, the family attribution will be waived. As a result of the waiver, the business owner may have his or her stock redeemed without the adverse tax consequences associated with the transaction being considered a dividend distribution.

Strategies for the Business Owner When the Business Is Transferred to Other Owners

When the business interest is being transferred to other non-family owners or to company employees, the private annuity and SCIN strategies examined are not usually appropriate. Their inappropriateness stems from the self-canceling nature of the SCIN and from the unsecured promise to make payments under the private annuity. That does not mean, however, that there are no strategies that can be implemented when the transfer is to a non-family member.

Depending upon the particular situation of the business owner, two strategies deserve examination. Those strategies are:

1. the installment sale; and

2. the charitable remainder trust.

We noted earlier that the retiring business owner often has two principal needs: providing a retirement income and minimizing taxes. Those needs exist for the business owner regardless of who the buyer is.

The Installment Sale. The sale of the business interest to other owners or to employees upon the retirement of the business owner is normally done from the selling business owner's perspective to:

- spread the reporting of any gain on the sale over the period in which installment payments of the purchase price are made; and

- provide retirement income.

To the extent that the installment sale accomplishes these two goals for the business owner, it has met, to some extent, the owner's needs. From the business buyer's point of view, the installment sale permits the buyer to spread the payments over an extended period of time and also use the income generated from the business to help make them.

The installment sale treatment is available for the corporate business interest provided the stock is not traded on an established securities market. In addition, the sale of a partnership interest can also qualify for installment sale treatment except to the extent of recapture income from depreciated partnership property or the business owner's share of inventory.

The advantages for the business owner of the installment sale include all of the following:

- The business owner receives a retirement income.

- The reportable gain on the sale is spread over the installment period rather than being recognized, in its entirety, in the same tax year. Each selling price installment is allocated between reportable gain and a tax-free return of basis.

- The promise to make payments is secured.

- The appreciation of the business is avoided for estate tax purposes.

Certain disadvantages of the installment sale should be stated. They are:

- The business owner may outlive his or her income from the installment sale.

- The balance of any payments due is included in the business owner's federal gross estate.

- An interest charge, payable to the IRS, is imposed on the tax that is deferred to the extent the amount of the obligation at the close of a year exceeds $5 million.

The tax benefits of the installment sale can be lost to the seller if the installment obligation is pledged as security for another loan. In that event, the proceeds of the loan are treated, for tax purposes, as a payment received on the installment note. As a result, the tax due is accelerated.

Although the installment sale has some benefits to both the buyer and the seller of the business interest, it is far from a panacea. A different approach, and one seldom considered by business owners, may meet more of the business owner's goals. Let's consider the charitable remainder trust strategy.

Charitable Remainder Trust Strategy

Using a *charitable remainder trust* strategy, the business owner makes a charitable contribution of his or her appreciated business to a charitable trust that the business owner has established. The trustee then sells the business and invests the funds.

During the lifetime of the business owner or the business owner and his or her spouse, the trust provides them with an income. At the business owner's death or upon the last of the business owner and spouse to die, the corpus of the trust is transferred to a charity.

To avoid the inheritance shrinkage that would result for the heirs from the charitable gift, an irrevocable life insurance trust is often established which purchases life insurance whose premium is paid for through non-charitable annual gifts. Upon the death of the business owner and the transfer of the trust corpus to the charitable remainderman, the life insurance is paid to the trust free of both income and estate taxes for subsequent distribution to the heirs.

The use of this strategy for the business owner of a highly appreciated business offers several advantages. Among these advantages are the following:

- The business owner or the business owner and his or her spouse achieve a lifetime retirement income. The income formula can be structured to provide either a fixed income for a fixed percentage of the trust assets. Wide latitude is permitted in determining the income level. The income provided must be at least 5 percent of the trust value and not more than 50 percent.

- The funds invested to provide the income are not depleted by any income or capital gains tax liability based on the appreciation of the business (as they would be if the business were sold by the business owner). The charitable trust is considered a charity for tax purposes and pays no income taxes.

- The business owner receives an income tax charitable deduction that may be used in the tax year in which the contribution was made, and any unused deduction may be carried over and used in any of the five succeeding tax years. The value of the charitable gift is the difference between the value of the gifted company and the present value of the income interest retained by the business owner, based on the business owner's or the business owner's and spouse's life expectancy.

- The value of the business is removed entirely from the business owner's federal gross estate.

- The value of the gifted property may be replaced through an irrevocable life insurance trust, often referred to as an "asset replacement trust."

In addition to the obvious financial benefits for the business owner that result from the charitable trust strategy, this strategy also gives the business owner the opportunity to benefit a charity that may be important to him or her. A number of variations to the general strategy employing the charitable trust exist, including the funding of a private charitable foundation. The private foundation, in addition to providing ongoing charitable gifts to many worthy causes, enables the business owner to provide a possible career to children as employees of the foundation.

The charitable trust strategy, although of substantial benefit in many situations, will not be appropriate in all cases. Some of the concerns in its use include:

- The business owner may be uninsurable and, as a result, may be unable to qualify for life insurance owned by the ILIT to replace the value of the charitable gift for his or her heirs. Although the three-year estate bringback rule may result in the inclusion in the estate of the business owner of the proceeds of an existing policy, policies owned by the business can be used in the event the business owner is uninsurable.

- The most appropriate business for the application of the charitable remainder trust strategy is one that has substantially appreciated and is wholly owned by the business owner. Partnerships or corporations in which co-stockholders have substantial holdings whose interest cannot be purchased are less likely to be appropriate candidates for this strategy.

Strategies for the Business

The principal goals for the business managed by its remaining business owners are simply stated and easily understood. They are:

- survival during the transition period; and

- eventual growth and profitability.

To meet these goals, we identified various steps that must be taken. In addition to ensuring that the business interest will not have to be sold to meet estate tax needs, those identified steps include:

- the need to locate, hire and develop competent successor management;

- the need to replace the key person business owner; and

- the need for sufficient cash to:

  - offset the economic loss usually suffered by the business after the loss of the key person;

  - bolster the company's financial picture for suppliers and customers; and

  - provide for the cost to replace the key person.

The important question is how each of these needs may be satisfied through the implementation of one or more business strategies. As we noted earlier, the departure of the business owner through retirement permits the business time to put the appropriate strategies in place as opposed to the crisis that could ensue if the departure was due to the business owner's death or disability. We will look at how each of the identified needs may be met and will find that, in large part, the successful strategy will depend on whether the business is to be retained in the family or transferred to other owners or employees.

Competent Successor Management

One of the vital needs for any business is competent management. For the family-retained business that means identifying, developing (and testing) and, eventually, selecting the appropriate successor. Ideally, more than one potential successor is identified.

We discussed the importance and methods of locating and hiring the right successor in Chapter 3, and a reiteration of that information may be of limited value. Of significant importance, however, is providing the candidates with as many opportunities as possible to learn the business and demonstrate their abilities. This often requires that the business owner suppress a natural desire to step in when the successor candidate makes mistakes. Equally important is the clear-eyed selection of the appropriate successor, and that may require the realization that a child of the business owner may not be the right person for the job.

In the case of the business transferred to current owners, the appropriate strategy often calls for the gradual assumption by the remaining owners of the management duties performed by the retiring business owner. This realignment of duties also requires an unbiased assessment of the owners' ability to competently handle these new tasks and a reassignment of them when the tasks' requirements are inconsistent with the talents, interests or skills of the owners asked to accomplish them.

Replacement of the Key Person

In the case of the family-retained business in which the successor has been identified, selected and trained, there may be less need to hire an additional employee to assume the duties of the retiring business owner *provided the management development has begun early enough*. The identified successor may be competent to assume them.

In those cases where the development of the successor has started late or, for some reason, has taken more time than anticipated, the business needs to consider the elevation of a current employee to the position of a second in command. The employee can then guide the still-developing family successor until he or she is fully competent to take on the overall management of the business.

If no current employee is available to fill the role of the interim assistant to the designated successor, the business may have to look to other companies in the industry. One or more of these other companies may have a competent executive looking for a change and willing to take on the duties of second in command in a family business.

In the business whose ownership is to be fully assumed by current owners, usually no additional management employee joins the firm and assumes the duties of the key person. The appropriate strategy may be to identify the skills, talents and duties that need to be replaced and those possessed by the current owners. The business, therefore, can identify the skills, contacts and so on that they seek in the key person's replacement and attain the skills and other requirements the business needs.

Additional Funds

Money may be the mother's milk of politics, but it plays just as big a role in helping to ensure business success. In fact, the leading cause of business failure is not ineffective management; it is a lack of funding. This need is far less the need for assets. It is the need for cash.

When we looked at the needs of the business, we saw that it had a need for sufficient cash to:

- offset the economic loss suffered by the business on the loss of the key person;

- strengthen the company's financial picture, generally, to give greater confidence to suppliers and customers; and

- locate and attract the departing business owner's replacement.

This cash requirement to ease the transition for the business upon the retirement of the business owner speaks volumes for the need to fund a stock redemption agreement and provide for the replacement of a deceased key person through permanent life insurance. The quickly available funds represented by cash values can go a long way in ensuring the successful transition.

Unfortunately, the cash values of business-owned life insurance alone may be insufficient to meet all of the business' needs during this period. For that reason, the business should consider a program of regular additions to retained earnings, beginning several years before the expected retirement, to provide a sinking fund to meet these expected and unexpected financial demands that are likely to follow upon the business owner's departure.

■ TRANSFER OF POLICY CASH VALUES TO THE RETIREE

The life insurance policies on the business owner's life are often no longer necessary when he or she retires. The question may arise concerning their disposition. The business' providing for the funding of various insurance needs during the business owner's tenure through permanent life insurance may mean that those policies have cash value that can assist in the lifetime buyout. Often, cash values on the retiring business owner's life are used to provide an initial down payment on the purchase price of the business. That can be done either through the surrender of the policies or through their transfer to the retiree. For the business, either choice—surrender or transfer—is usually acceptable. The choice, however, may make a big difference to the business owner.

Personal Use of Business-Owned Policies

The three issues that often control the business owner's desire to obtain the corporate life insurance policies intact are:

1. the need for personally owned life insurance to meet various requirements, including:

   - the cost-effective payment of estate liabilities such as taxes, probate costs and various professional fees;

   - the replacement of spousal income in the case of the use of a private annuity or SCIN;

   - the replacement of the value of the business for the heirs in the employment of a charitable remainder trust strategy; or

   - many other uses;

2. his or her possible uninsurability; and

3. the significantly higher premiums that may be required for new life insurance because of his or her age.

Regardless of the nature of the business owner's personal financial need, existing corporate-owned life insurance can play an important role in filling it.

Transfer for Value Not a Problem

One of the concerns that we have come to recognize in the transfer of the ownership of life insurance policies in return for something else relates to the *transfer-for-value rule*. Briefly, the transfer-for-value rule provides that the general exemption from income taxation of life insurance death benefit proceeds does not apply in those cases where the policy has been sold or otherwise transferred for a value consideration.

In the case of a policy transferred for value, the death benefit will avoid income taxation only to the extent of the consideration paid by the transferee plus any subsequent net premiums paid by the transferee. In other words, any "profit" that the individual purchasing the policy realizes is income taxable as ordinary income under the transfer-for-value rule. Fortunately, specific exceptions apply to the situation involving the business owner.

Although several exceptions to the transfer-for-value rule exist, the only exception that we need to be aware of in this case concerns the transfer of the insurance policy to the insured. Under the exceptions to the transfer-for-value rule recited in Section 101(a)(2)(B) of the Internal Revenue Code, the income tax exception is available despite the sale or other transfer for value if the sale or other transfer for value is to the insured himself or herself.

So, despite the need for caution in transfering life insurance policy ownership in return for consideration, we need not be concerned when the transfer of the life insurance policy is to the insured business owner.

Estate Inclusion May Be an Issue

One of the substantial tax problems that many successful business owners have concerns estate taxes. An estate of a business owner with assets in excess of $3 million may find that 55 percent of the estate must be paid in taxes. Life insurance, often successfully employed to meet those estate liabilities, may sometimes make the estate tax problem worse by increasing the value of the estate.

Under Section 2042 of the Internal Revenue Code, a decedent's gross estate includes the value of life insurance proceeds on the decedent's life that are payable to:

- the decedent's estate; or

- others from life insurance policies over which the decedent had any incidents of ownership at the time of his or her death.

In addition, the death benefit proceeds of a life insurance policy in which the decedent had any incidents of ownership at any time within the three years prior to his or her death will also be brought back into the estate for tax purposes under the "bringback rule."

Because the death benefit proceeds payable under any life insurance policy that the business owner owned during the three years prior to his or her death are brought back into the estate, the use of corporate-owned life insurance is a potential problem.

If life insurance policies owned by the business on the life of the retiring business owner are transferred to him or her for any reason, it could spell trouble. Even if the policy was in partial payment for the business, that ownership—even if momentary—is sufficient. The result is that the death benefits will be included in the business owner's estate in the event of death within three years after a subsequent transfer of ownership to a trust or other owner.

ILL. 5.2 ■ *Look Out for the Bringback Rule*

Using that $1 million life insurance policy that you own to fund an irrevocable life insurance trust may not be the answer to the problem. If the insured owned the policy at any time during the three years before his or her death, the death benefit proceeds will be considered a part of the insured's estate for tax purposes, and that could add up to an additional $550,000 to your estate tax bill!

Transferring corporate-owned life insurance may be the only way that the uninsurable business owner can get it. If your client faces this situation, you should be sure to fully disclose the possible estate tax consequences of his or her ownership. Alternatively, if the business owner can qualify for life insurance and estate taxes are a concern, he or she should consider establishing an irrevocable life insurance trust and having it purchase new insurance on his or her life to meet estate liquidity or other needs.

■ TAX AND ESTATE PLANNING ISSUES

The principal tax and estate planning issues that may arise on the retirement of the business owner are generally the providing of retirement income, the minimizing of various taxes and arranging for their cost-effective payment.

If the transfer is by an inter vivos gift to a family member, the primary concern may be minimizing gift taxes. A strategy that may be employed to help reduce the extent of gift taxes is the grantor retained trust. If the transfer of business interest is the result of a sale to a family owner, the use of strategies such as a self-canceling installment note or a private annuity may be appropriate. In both strategies, the beneficial results include providing a retirement income, reducing income taxes on the gain by spreading the payment over a number of years and reducing estate taxes.

Transfers to non-family members can be accomplished through the use of a charitable remainder trust to accomplish the goals of providing retirement income and tax minimization. If, for some reason, the charitable remainder trust strategy is inappropriate, an installment note purchase can help spread the reportable gain on the sale over the lifetime of the note.

The use of an irrevocable life insurance trust to purchase and own life insurance on the business owner's life can provide funds with which to satisfy estate liabilities without causing the death benefit proceeds to increase the size of the federal gross estate.

■ RETIREMENT SUCCESSION AND RETIREMENT PLANS

We noted earlier in this chapter that one of the principal needs of the retiring business owner was for income in retirement. It is often with that need in mind that the business owner plans for the transfer of his or her business interest. While the creation of additional retirement income from the sale of the business is a worthwhile objective, the overriding need to create an income from that source may limit the business transfer options available to the business owner.

The intra-family sales that we examined earlier provide an example. It seems clear that the retiring business owner, in addition to assuring an adequate retirement income and minimizing the tax impact of the transfer, also has a stake in the business' continued prosperity. To some extent, his or her satisfaction of one of the goals may be at odds with the satisfaction of another.

One of the concerns in the implementation of either the private annuity or self-canceling installment note strategies is that the financial burden assumed by the successor family member may have an adverse effect on the success of the business.

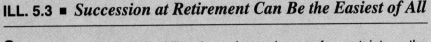

ILL. 5.3 ■ *Succession at Retirement Can Be the Easiest of All*

Succession at death or disability always has a degree of uncertainty — the timing is generally unknowable and the departed owner is unavailable for assistance. Succession at retirement can be a much smoother process.

Successor taking over the reins of the business after the retirement of the owner

Furthermore, the purchaser's cost basis may be limited to his or her payments actually made. In either case, that cost basis—because payments terminate at the death of the annuitant—may be very modest. As a result, a subsequent sale of the business interest may have enormous capital gains consequences.

However, if retirement income for the business owner was not a concern, the business could be retained by the business owner during his or her retirement and bequeathed to the heirs at death. The result would be a greater likelihood of business success because it would not be burdened by buyout payments and a stepped-up basis equal to the market value of the business at death for the heirs.

Retirement plans generally fall into two general categories: qualified plans and non-qualified plans. The fundamental distinction relates to qualification. Qualified retirement plans "qualify" for favorable tax treatment, including before-tax contributions and tax deferral of plan earnings until they are distributed; non-qualified plans do not.

The major tax advantages of a qualified retirement plan are as follows:

- contributions to the plan are currently deductible;

- employees (including the self-employed) can defer taxation on accumulated amounts until they are distributed to them;

- lump-sum distributions are subject to special income averaging provisions and may be rolled over to an IRA or to other qualified plans;

- under certain circumstances, distributions may qualify for a retirement income credit; and

- distributions may be subject to a lower income tax rate than the rate that would have been imposed had the income been taxable at the time of the employer's contribution to the plan.

In return for favorable tax treatment, qualified plans must meet an extensive number of rules, including non-discrimination rules. The non-discrimination rules require, in general, that the business not exclude employees. Those regulations and the requirement that, generally, the plan must cover all employees result in significant costs for the small business. Plan costs and the administration required have, in the past, kept many small businesses from establishing a qualified retirement plan.

Non-qualified plans enjoy few of the tax benefits that are common in qualified plans. However, non-qualified plans have three important benefits for the company. Those benefits are that:

- Non-qualified plans are exempt from ERISA regulation with the exception of certain disclosure and reporting requirements.

- Non-qualified plans are permitted to discriminate in favor of highly compensated employees. That permitted discrimination may allow the business to establish a retirement plan for the business owner alone.

- The business may recover all or part of its costs to provide the non-qualified plan benefits.

In addition to allowing the business to provide an income to the retiring business owner, a non-qualified deferred compensation plan can be used by the company to attract key employees, including a replacement for the retiring business owner. However, if the qualified retirement plan has disadvantages in cost and administration, the non-qualified plan has one significant disadvantage.

The principal disadvantage is that the promised benefits under a non-qualified plan are frequently unsecured. Because many non-qualified plans are unfunded, the business owner may find that the non-qualified plan that was to help fund his or her retirement may provide nothing at all if the business falls into financial difficulty when promised benefits are due.

As with so many of the strategies and techniques that we have examined, no one method is the best in every case. It depends on the situations of both the business and the business owner.

■ CASE STUDY: BIGBUCKS MANUFACTURING

Bill Bigbucks is within six months of retiring from Bigbucks Manufacturing, and he is pleased to see that his daughter Susan has assumed virtually all of the major management responsibilities at Bigbucks. All that remains is to transfer the business to his daughter.

The current value of the business is estimated to be $2,150,000 and includes the following assets:

	Current Value
Equipment	$750,000
Inventory	$150,000
Accounts receivable	$200,000
Other assets	$50,000
Total balance sheet asset	$1,150,000
Patents	$1,000,000
Total assets	$2,150,000

Bill's personal balance sheet, once the business was transferred to Susan, would look as follows:

Assets		Liabilities	
Home	$575,000	Home mortgage	$225,000
Personal property	$75,000	Burial and final expenses	$10,000
Securities	$150,000	Estate administration	$5,000
IRA	$200,000	Policy loan	$25,000
Life insurance	$85,000	Other debts	$12,500
Value of the business	$0	Inheritance tax	$5,000
Total	$1,085,000		$282,500

In addition to these assets, Bill has created an irrevocable life insurance trust that owns life insurance in the amount of $2,370,357 and which can provide an income for Bill's wife Beth upon his death.

Bill's Concerns

Because Beth's income upon Bill's death is provided for, Bill is only concerned with:

- providing an income for himself at retirement;

- reducing his estate taxes (which would occur once the business was transferred to Susan); and

- reducing the income taxes for which he would be liable upon the sale of the business.

The Solution

To transfer the business at Bill's retirement to his daughter, Susan, they enter into a private annuity agreement. Under the private annuity agreement, Bill receives an income of $265,000 annually for his lifetime, which satisfies Bill's goal for retirement income.

Upon Bill's death, the payments cease. Beth's income would, of course, be provided through the life insurance owned by the irrevocable life insurance trust which would be payable upon Bill's death.

Income taxes on the sale are minimized because the capital gains income that Bill would be required to recognize would be spread over the payments received, provided that the promise to pay is not secured. Finally, the estate taxes would be reduced because the business and its value had been transferred to Susan in return for the unsecured promise to pay the periodic private annuity payments to her father. Bill has kept the business in the family, provided a retirement income for himself, eliminated estate taxes and reduced his capital gain on the sale of the business interest.

■ SUMMARY

This chapter examined the needs of the business owner and the business at the business owner's retirement. We saw that the needs of the business owner were principally to provide income during retirement and to minimize income, gift and estate taxes. The needs of the business that were discussed centered on initial business survival and ultimate profitability. The needs discussed included successor management, key person replacement and cash. We then examined the strategies that can be implemented to meet those needs.

The tax and estate planning issues incident to succession at retirement were discussed. They were determined to be principally estate, gift and income tax minimization. Finally, the role of qualified and non-qualified retirement plans in facilitating the retirement of the owner and the success of the business was addressed.

■ **CHAPTER 5 QUESTIONS FOR REVIEW**

1. What usually is considered to be the most important need that business owners have upon transfer of their business interest at retirement?

    A. Obtain income

    B. Reduce taxes

    C. Increase assets

    D. Decrease assets

2. Which of the following is usually the most serious problem faced by the estate of the deceased business owner?

    A. Too much uninvested cash

    B. Too few assets

    C. Poor liquidity

    D. Substantial probate costs

3. All of the following are considered to be important business needs occasioned by the business owner's retirement EXCEPT

    A. the need to find competent successor management

    B. the need to replace a key person

    C. the need for additional cash

    D. the need to increase cost basis

4. Why may a private annuity be considered an inappropriate arrangement for the sale of the business interest to other than family members?

    A. The income provided to the business owner would be insufficient.

    B. The promise to pay the annuity income is unsecured and, therefore, represents greater risk.

    C. The business owner would be liable for gift taxes.

    D. The gain on the sale of the business interest would be due immediately.

5. Why would the transfer of a business-owned life insurance policy to the insured business owner NOT result in a transfer for value problem?

    A. The cash value is usually fully borrowed by the business before the policy is transferred to the insured.

    B. There would be no recognizable gain on the policy.

    C. The sale or other transfer for value to the insured him- or herself is a specific exception to the transfer-for-value rule.

    D. Business-owned policies are specifically exempted from the transfer-for-value rule.

6

Valuing the Business

W hat is a business worth? Is it the total of the assets on its books, less its liabilities? Some function of its earnings? The value that a buyer and seller agree to give it? If you offered any of these answers, you may be partly correct and partly incorrect. The answer is "it depends."

The practitioner seeking a method of determining a precise valuation formula is bound to be disappointed. Business valuation is anything but an exact science. The fact is that valuing a business interest is, at best, an imprecise art. Despite this imprecision, the Internal Revenue Code imposes a valuation standard. The standard for value, according to the Code, is:

> *The price at which the property would change hands between a willing buyer and a willing seller, neither being under any compulsion to buy and sell and both having reasonable knowledge of relevant facts.*

In the chapter ahead of us, we will examine various methods that can be used to value a business. We will also see that different methods may be better suited to particular kinds of business or situations. Finally, we will talk about how the selection of the valuation method is incorporated into the plan.

Chapter Objectives

In this chapter, you will learn:

- the common methods of business valuation;

- the discounts that may apply in a particular client's situation;

- how to evaluate the appropriateness of a particular valuation method for use in particular situations; and

- how the valuation method is incorporated into the succession plan.

■ ■ ■ ■ ■

■ METHODS OF BUSINESS VALUATION

We should emphasize that after using one or more of the methods of business valuation that we will be examining, all we will have is an approximation of the value of the business. Unfortunately, the precision with which the methods are stated and explained may give the erroneous impression that the result is as exact as the method. It isn't.

As we discuss the various methods by which a business can be valued, keep in mind that certain methods may be inherently less valuable because of the accounting conventions on which they are based. Other methods may provide a better approximation of value for a particular type of business. Remember, however, that even though certain methods may afford better approximations, they are still approximations.

We will be looking at seven approaches to establishing business value. Those approaches are:

1. book value

2. capitalization of earnings

3. straight capitalization

4. years purchase method

5. appraisal value

6. agreed value

7. discounted cash flow

Realizing that business valuation formulas may give us less certainty than we might hope for, let's turn our attention to the formulas themselves.

Book Value

Starting with the *book value* seems to make some sense for two reasons. First, for the uninitiated, the simple act of subtracting liabilities from assets would seem to give us the worth of the organization. After all, that approach works for us as individuals. Second, book value may be viewed as a starting place—in a sense, a jumping-off point—for a discussion of how to establish a value for any business.

ILL. 6.1 ■ *From Revenue Ruling 59-60*

"**O**ften, an appraiser will find wide differences of opinion as to the fair market value of a particular stock. In resolving such differences, he or she should maintain a reasonable attitude in light of the fact that valuation is not an exact science."

The term "book value" refers to the business valuation being made by reference to the books of the business. While book value is a common method used for establishing the value of stock to be purchased, possibly because of its simplicity, it should not be considered the final word in fixing value. It simply has too many deficiencies. If it has a value in the job of business valuation, it may be as a check on other valuation methods or a starting point when other methods fail to provide a meaningful valuation.

Establishing the book value of any business requires the following:

Total assets are determined	Assets	$1,500,000
Total liabilities are subtracted	– Liabilities	– $675,000
The result is the book value	Book Value	$825,000

The calculation is certainly simple enough. Let's consider why book value may be of limited value. To do that, we need to understand where the numbers come from, and what they reflect and don't reflect.

A business' assets and liabilities are shown on its balance sheet. The value of any asset on the balance sheet is its acquisition cost less any depreciation taken by the company. (Depreciation, of course, reflects the wearing out of an asset.)

To understand why this depreciated value of the asset may be unreliable for our purposes, consider the situation in which a business has only one asset. That asset, shown on the balance sheet, is an office building purchased five years before a major urban renewal effort took place in the area adjacent to the building. Depreciation rules permit the building to be depreciated over a 31.5 year period. If the cost of the building (not the land) was $10 million, each year the business could value it at $317,460 less than the previous year ($10,000,000 ÷ 31.5 = $317,460).

As a result of that depreciation, the building's value shown on the company's books at the end of the five-year period is $8,412,698. The value of the building has been reduced by $1,587,302, representing five years of depreciation. Because of the urban renewal effort, the value of the office building may have doubled and could now be worth $20 million. Assuming that the business had only one liability—the $750,000 mortgage—the company's book value would be $250,000. However, we know that the actual value of the business may be much closer to $10,250,000! The book value fails to show appreciation in value and carries assets at their cost less depreciation.

Another reason why book value may be unreliable in any particular situation is because it often does not reflect the value of intangible assets such as goodwill, patents and copyrights, marketing lists, etc. To the extent that a business has intangible assets, the book value approach to valuation becomes increasingly inappropriate. A personal services business, for example, would not be one whose value could be approximated using the book value approach. If there is any type of business that might be able to use this method, it is one comprised primarily of inventory and with few other assets.

Capitalization of Earnings

The *capitalization of earnings* approach adds the value of goodwill to the book value of the business. For purposes of examining this approach to valuing the business, let's assume that ABC Distributing, Inc. is a closely held corporation with the following financial numbers:

Total earnings last five years	$800,000
Book value	$150,000

The formula for the capitalization of earnings valuation is:

1. Average annual earnings in last five years	$160,000
2. Less assumed return on book value (7 percent assumed)	–$10,500
3. Excess earnings (not attributable to company assets)	$149,500
4. Multiply by the goodwill factor (see table below)	× 4
5. Total value of goodwill	$598,000
6. Add the book value	+$150,000
7. Total value of the business (book value plus goodwill)	$748,000

You will notice in step 4 above that the earnings that are attributable to goodwill ($149,500) are multiplied by a goodwill factor that has been deemed to be 4. The goodwill factor deserves some explanation.

The goodwill factor is a multiplier based on the business type and is a measure of the business' ability to generate income beyond the life of its owners. The factors that are often used as a multiplier are shown below for the various business types.

Business Type	Goodwill Factor
Personal service businesses	1 – 2
Closely held businesses	3 – 4
Medium-size, well-established businesses	5 – 7
Public corporations	8 – 15

Certain types of businesses should not be valued using the capitalization of earnings valuation method because it would tend to give a distorted value. It may be inappropriate in a business where assets aren't a factor of valuation. For example, a personal service business may have very few assets but may possess a valuable client list. The client list, of course, would not be included in the balance sheet. With such a business, the next valuation approach—straight capitalization—may be more appropriate.

Straight Capitalization

The *straight capitalization* approach to business valuation uses a somewhat simpler approach than the capitalization of earnings method that we just examined. In the straight capitalization method, total average annual earnings are capitalized rather than the excess earnings attributable to goodwill as in the last formula. The capitalization rate that is used in this approach to valuation depends upon how likely the business is to outlive its owner.

Before looking at the formula, let's consider the capitalization rates that are used with the various business types. When reviewing the capitalization rates, remember that the lower the rate, the higher the business valuation.

Business Type	Capitalization Rate
Old established businesses with very large capital assets and substantial goodwill. Generally few businesses are in this category.	10%
Well-established businesses with considerable stability and, largely, insulated from general economic conditions. May include most old, successful businesses.	12.5%
Well-established businesses with products that render them vulnerable to economic downturn. Requires considerable managerial ability but relatively little specialized knowledge.	15%
Businesses requiring average managerial ability and relatively small capital. Will generally have established goodwill but will be competing in a highly competitive industry. This category includes most medium-size companies.	20%
Generally small businesses in very competitive industries. Little capital required. Protected by few barriers to entry by others.	25%
Businesses (large or small) that depend on the unique skill of a small group of managers. Failure rate is high.	50%
Personal services businesses. Little or no capital required, but owner must have intensive and thorough knowledge of business. Cannot be sold without a manager.	100%

Let's return to our fictitious firm, ABC Distributing, Inc., and value it using the formula for straight capitalization. As we indicated earlier, ABC is a closely held corporation with the following financial numbers with total five-year earnings of

$800,000 and a book value of $150,000. With the financial numbers shown, ABC may fall into the above category with a 20 percent capitalization rate.

The formula for the straight capitalization valuation is:

Average annual earnings in last five years	$160,000
Divided by the capitalization factor	÷ .20
Total business value	$800,000

Although no absolutely perfect valuation method exists for any type of business, the straight capitalization method of business valuation would seem to be of particular application in a company owning a highly valued intangible asset. Because the asset is intangible, it may not be included on any financial statement. As a result, book value would seem to have even less application in such a case.

Years Purchase Method

Let's use ABC Distributing Company's financial numbers again to see how the *years purchase* method approach values it. The formula for the years purchase method of valuation is:

1. Average annual earnings in last five years	$160,000
2. Less assumed return on book value (7 percent assumed)	–$10,500
3. Excess earnings (not attributable to company assets)	$149,500
4. Multiply by three years	× 3
5. Total excess earnings	$448,500
6. Add the book value	+$150,000
7. Total value (book value plus excess earnings)	$598,500

The years purchase method is designed to more accurately measure the value of non-asset factors. These non-asset factors are represented by the earnings in excess of those earnings that would have resulted from the investment of the company's assets alone.

Appraisal Value

To establish a value that is most likely to successfully weather a challenge by the Internal Revenue Service, the business should be valued by an experienced appraiser. While the accounting firm that the business customarily uses immediately comes to mind, there may be some question as to whether that would be the proper choice. Although an accountant may be the best choice to appraise the book value of the business, he or she may not be the best judge of the goodwill associated with it.

In valuing a business, the professional appraiser is customarily guided by Revenue Ruling 59-60. In this ruling, the Internal Revenue Service provides the appraiser with eight factors that must be considered in the valuation of closely held businesses. These eight factors are:

1. *History and nature of the business.* This would include the business' prospects for growth, its risks and diversity as well as its product lines, management performance, geographical diversity, capital structure, and adequacy of property, plan and equipment.

2. *Industry and general economic outlook.* This would include an evaluation of the competition and an appraisal of the business being valued compared with others within the same industry.

3. *Book value and financial condition.* This factor calls for the evaluation of the business balance sheet and its nonoperating assets.

4. *Earning capacity.* Appraisers need to examine the company's profit and loss and cash flow statements to assess this factor.

5. *Dividend-paying capacity.* This is considered by the IRS to be less significant than the other factors. In evaluating this factor, the appraiser needs to look at the business' capacity to pay dividends rather than its history of paying dividends.

6. *Existence of goodwill or other intangible value.* This factor is evaluated by determining the company's earnings in excess of the earnings that would be attributable to its net tangible assets.

7. *Prior sales and the size of the block of stock.*

8. *Comparisons to similar publicly traded companies.*

Normally when the appraisal value is used as the method of establishing price, the parties agree that the value of the business will be established by an appraisal made within a specified time after the date on which it becomes necessary to fix the price. The principal decision that must be made is to identify the appraiser.

Agreed Value

Under the *agreed value* method of establishing the business value, the parties fix the actual purchase price that will appear in the buy-sell agreement at the time of entering into the agreement. Because the business value tends to change over time, the agreement customarily provides for revision on an annual basis and more frequently if circumstances warrant.

If it is anticipated that there will be frequent revisions in the agreed value, the agreement may provide that, upon failure to revise the value in accordance with the agreement, the value will be fixed by taking the most recent stated amount as a base and adjusting it for any subsequent changes in book value as determined by the accountants.

The stated price method has four primary advantages:

1. There is no misunderstanding as to the agreed-upon value. Because there is no formula that may be incompletely comprehended, there is little likelihood that a party to the agreement will not understand.

2. The parties to the agreement, knowing the exact price at which their share of the business will be purchased, can do the necessary estate planning with confidence.

3. Knowing the exact price makes it easier to be certain that the full price is insured.

4. The transfer of the business is simplified.

Two disadvantages normally are associated with the agreed value approach to valuation. The first disadvantage is that this method does not reflect changes that occur between valuation restatements. The second disadvantage is that the parties must agree on a value of the business each year.

Discounted Cash Flow

The *discounted cash flow* approach to valuing a business represents a newer and somewhat more sophisticated model of business valuation. Its use is consistent with the Internal Revenue Service's emphasis in its valuation guidelines on cash flow.

Under the discounted cash flow method, the business value is equivalent to the future expected cash flow discounted at a rate that reflects the risks associated with achieving the cash flow results. Valuation recognizes that, from an investment perspective, the actual cash produced by a business and returned to the investor may be more attractive to purchasers than business earnings that may not be converted to cash. It acknowledges that the basis of any business' worth is cash flow.

To determine the value of a business under the discounted cash flow method, the cash flow that is expected to be generated from the company's activities is analyzed and adjusted. The future cash flows of the business are determined by projecting the company's annual earnings over the forecast period. That projection is done by examining the company's past earnings, expected net earnings from its major contracts, and future capital expenditures. These earnings are then adjusted to approximate cash flow.

Once anticipated cash flow is determined for the forecast period, it is discounted to its present value using a rate that reflects the risk involved in the investment. The final value is based on the value of any assets that are expected to exist at the end of the forecast period. The value of these assets are also discounted to present value. The two present values are then added together to obtain the value of the business.

The discounted cash flow approach to valuation seems to be more consistent with the views of the IRS concerning the importance of future cash flow in valuing a business. However, because of its relative sophistication, it may give the impression that it is the final answer to the knotty problem of business valuation. Don't be fooled; despite its general complexity and greater sophistication, the result obtained is still an approximation.

Now that we have examined the methods used to determine the value of a business, we need to look at those factors that reflect the nature of the client with which we may be dealing. Many of our business clients will be owners of closely held businesses. By definition, these are businesses that are not listed on an exchange. In other words, the client can't call his or her stockbroker and quickly sell those shares.

ILL. 6.2 ■ *From Revenue Ruling 59-60*

"No formula can be devised that will be generally applicable to the multitude of different valuation issues arising in estate and gift tax cases . . . A sound valuation will be based upon all relevant facts but the element of common sense, informed judgment and reasonableness must enter into the process of weighing those facts and determining their aggregate significance."

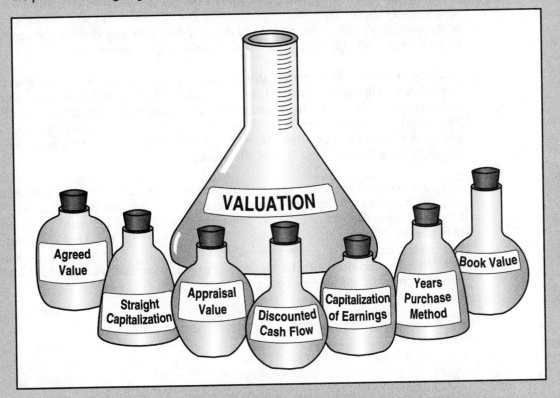

Nonmarketability and Minority Interest Discounts

The methods that we have examined for valuing a business are useful in arriving at an approximation of the worth of an entire business. But, what if the value of the client's interest in the business is one-half or one-third of the entire business? Is the value of his or her portion one-half or one-third, respectively, of the entire business? The answer is "probably not." We will look at the issue of minority interests immediately after we examine the problem that is endemic in almost all closely-held businesses: nonmarketability.

Having the ability to quickly liquidate a business interest has a value. Conversely, the inability to do so reduces the value of the interest. That is the fundamental issue of *nonmarketability*. When a business interest is nonmarketable, a discounted value may be assigned to it.

Nonmarketability.   The fact that an established market does not exist for stock in a closely held corporation or for a partnership interest seriously affects the marketability of the business interest. That lack of marketability exists whether the business owner has a minority or majority interest in the business. As a result, the courts have allowed a discount for the lack of marketability of both controlling interests and minority interests.

Although the appropriate discount for lack of marketability is difficult to determine, at least one study* has concluded that a 35 percent nonmarketability discount from intrinsic value is appropriate for stock in a closely held corporation. In view of the similarity, in regard to nonmarketability of a partnership interest, arguably such a discount may apply to the general partnership as well. Not unlike so many elements of the valuation process, the amount of this discount also may depend upon other factors, such as whether the interest is a minority or controlling one.

Minority Interest.   The discount that may apply due to lack of marketability is different from the discount for a *minority interest*. In both the closely held corporation and the partnership, the holder of a minority interest occupies a precarious position. The minority business owner is not in a position to control salaries, distributions or policy. Because of this an otherwise willing buyer is likely to find the minority interest to be a risky and nonmarketable investment.

The minority stockholder or partner is frequently at the mercy of those holding a majority interest in the business. Because control rests with the majority stakeholder, whether that is a stockholder or partner, the holder of the minority interest may be excluded from managerial decisions. Because of that, those holding controlling interest can adversely affect the value of the minority holding. As a result of these adverse conditions affecting holders of minority interest, a discount similar to that for nonmarketability may be applicable.

---

* J. Michael Maher, *Discounts for Lack of Marketability for Closely Held Business Interests*, 54 Taxes 571 (1976).

▪ EVALUATING VALUATION METHODS IN PARTICULAR SITUATIONS

With all of the valuation methods available to help the client place a value on his or her business, what method should any business use? Although it can be argued that each valuation method has certain drawbacks and shortcomings, is there a specific method that is indicated for particular situations? These are reasonable questions, and, although there is no method that is right for all businesses and all situations, there are specific situations in which particular approaches to valuation are indicated.

In our examination of valuation methods, we saw that—except for the appraisal value and the agreed value approaches—they were each based on specific financial factors. Those factors were:

- tangible assets

- earnings

- cash flow

Selection of the valuation method that is likely to result in the closest approximation of the true business value requires an understanding of the principal factor that drives the success of the business. The valuation methods that we examined earlier and the factors on which they are based align themselves as follows:

Solely Asset Based	Book value
Assets and Earnings Based	Capitalization of earnings Years purchase method
Solely Earnings Based	Straight Capitalization
Cash Flow Based	Discounted cash flow

A business may be successful principally because of one person, and it may owe its earnings level to the particular talents or contacts of a specific individual. Where the business income is a function of the skills and expertise of a specific individual, it is unreasonable to value the business by reference to that income if it is the departure of that individual that brings about the need for valuation. In other words, if the income is solely the result of the individual, the death or disability of the individual will mean the end of that income. To the extent that the income declines, so does the value. In such a case, valuation should rely more heavily on the assets of the business.

When a personal service business is successful because of a single individual, the death, disability or retirement of that individual may mean that the business will no longer be successful. Accordingly, the value of the business after the departure of the individual should be based on the book value of the company (adjusted to reflect the fair market value of the assets) rather than the business earnings or cash flow.

A business may owe its success to a combination of its tangible assets and the skills of its owners. If the departure of one of its owners would not cripple the business, it would be reasonable to use a valuation approach that recognizes both factors. In that case the capitalization of earnings or years purchase method may be most appropriate because they use both excess earnings and earnings based on assets in their formulas.

Certain businesses owe their success to highly valued intangible assets, such as client lists, patents and copyrights rather than to either the talents of a single individual or to a wealth of tangible assets. Valuation of a business whose earnings are principally a function of those intangible assets is more likely to be adequately approximated using the straight capitalization method of valuation.

Finally, the discounted cash flow method of business valuation would seem to be most appropriate in those cases in which a business has contracts extending into the future that are expected to provide a substantial portion of company revenues. Although the anticipated residual value of tangible assets remaining at the end of the cash flow forecast period plays a role in valuation, cash flow is its primary determinant.

Let's return to the questions that we posed at the beginning of this section. You may remember that they were:

- "What valuation method should a business use?" and

- "Is there a specific method that is indicated for particular situations?"

The answers to those questions are similar to the question as to the superiority of any particular valuation method. The answer to that question is contained in the words of Revenue Ruling 59-60:

> *No formula can be devised that will be generally applicable to the multitude of different valuation issues arising in estate and gift tax cases. . . . A sound valuation will be based upon all relevant facts but the element of common sense, informed judgment and reasonableness must enter into the process of weighing those facts and determining their aggregate significance.*

The most important element in the selection of an appropriate valuation method is also contained in the ruling. It just may be common sense.

■ INCORPORATING THE VALUATION METHOD IN THE PLAN

That the individuals who are parties to the buy-sell agreement agree on a method of valuing the business is, obviously, important. It is no more important, however, than that the agreed-upon method become a part of the agreement itself. The reason for that is simple: the signed agreement stipulates and governs the specifics of the transaction. Furthermore, in many cases, one of the parties to the agreement will be dead and unable to explain what he or she understood.

The valuation method is incorporated into the buy-sell agreement through the purchase price provision. Let's look at various provisions that make the method a part of the agreement.

Agreed Value

The simplest method is the agreed value. A sample provision incorporating the agreed value in the buy-sell agreement for a partnership might be in a schedule appended to the agreement and read as shown below:

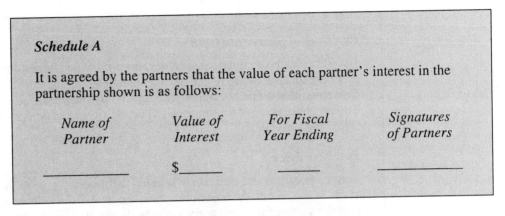

Schedule A

It is agreed by the partners that the value of each partner's interest in the partnership shown is as follows:

Name of Partner	*Value of Interest*	*For Fiscal Year Ending*	*Signatures of Partners*
_____	$_____	_____	_____

Each fiscal year, the value of the interest would be amended or affirmed, and a new Schedule A would be signed by each of the partners and appended to the buy-sell agreement. For valuation methods other than the agreed value approach, the provision is generally included in the body of the agreement rather than in a schedule.

Appraisal Value

Using the appraisal value method requires, of course, that a professional appraiser be used. So that parties to the buy-sell agreement may feel their interests are represented, the provision incorporated in the agreement may call for the average of the appraisal values determined by an appraiser chosen by each party—in this case the stockholder and the company—as in the provision below.

Agreement Price

The agreement price shall be the fair market value of the offered stock on the date of its offer or deemed offer.

How Computed

The agreement price shall be the average of the fair market value of the offered stock as determined by the qualified appraisers selected by the offering stockholder and by the Company.

The fair market value of the offered stock shall be determined under the same methods as would be used for determining the estate tax value of the offered stock if the offering stockholder had died on the date of the offer or deemed offer, ignoring any alternate valuation date or special use valuation. The Company shall provide such data as either of the qualified appraisers deems necessary or useful to make such determination of the fair market value of the offered stock.

Adjusted Book Value

The obvious deficiencies of the book value approach to business valuation can be overcome somewhat by adjusting it for goodwill as in the case of the cross purchase buy-sell provision shown below.

Purchase of Shares at Death

Upon the death of either shareholder, the surviving shareholder shall purchase and the estate of the decedent shall sell all of the shares of the Company now owned or hereafter acquired by the deceased shareholder. The purchase price of the shares shall be their value as determined under the following provision.

Purchase Price

The purchase price of each share is equal to the book value of the Company's assets at the end of the month in which the death of the shareholder occurs, plus the value of the Company's goodwill, divided by the number of shares then outstanding.

The value of the Company's goodwill shall be determined by multiplying by 7 the excess of:

A. its average annual net profits for the five complete fiscal years immediately preceding the date of death

B. 10 percent of its average annual net worth as at the end of the same periods

The calculation of the purchase price will be made by the Company's certified public accountant and such calculation shall be conclusive for all purposes.

Straight Capitalization (Limited by Book Value)

In this variation of the straight capitalization method of business valuation, the upper and lower limits of the value are determined by the book value. Such a cross-purchase buy-sell agreement provision might read as shown below.

Whether the valuation method chosen for the buy-sell agreement is one of the methods that we have examined or another, it is critical that it be recited in the agreement itself. Failure to include a provision similar to those shown in this section could leave the buyout transaction without a method to value the business interest.

Purchase of Shares at Death

Upon the death of either shareholder, the surviving shareholder shall purchase and the estate of the decedent shall sell all of the shares in the Company owned by the decedent at the date of death. The purchase price of the shares shall be their value as determined under the following provision.

Purchase Price

The value of the Company's shares is an amount equal to two times the aggregate of its net profits (after taxes) for the five completed fiscal years preceding the death of the shareholder whose shares are to be purchased. In no event, however, shall the value be an amount greater than 200 percent, nor less than 50 percent, of the book value of the shares as of the date of the shareholder's death.

The value of each share shall equal the value computed in accordance with the above provisions divided by the number of outstanding shares. The net profit or net loss for any fiscal year of the Company shall be the net income or net loss as shown on its federal income tax return for that year, except that capital gains or losses shall be computed at 100 percent, no adjustment shall be made for loss carrybacks or carryovers, and no account shall be taken of any changes in income or loss made by an amended return, by the Internal Revenue Service or the courts.

In determining the book value of the shares, the books of the Company shall be controlling. For this purpose, the last regular audit of the books prepared by the Company's certified public accountant shall be accepted as correct and shall be adjusted by the accountant for the operations from the date of the audit to the date of the shareholder's death. As to the value of the Company's shares, the accountant's certified determination shall be conclusive for all purposes.

■ **CASE STUDY: VALUING BIGBUCKS MANUFACTURING**

Bill Bigbucks' interest in Bigbucks Manufacturing is being purchased by his daughter, Susan, under a private annuity agreement. In order to ensure that no portion of the transaction is considered a gift by the IRS, it is important to establish a value for the business that will not be considered less than its true value. Because the value of the company is derived from a combination of its assets and non-assets, Bill and Susan have agreed to value the company under the years purchase method which recognizes both earnings sources.

Bigbucks Manufacturing's assets are as follows:

	Current Value
Equipment	$750,000
Inventory	$150,000
Accounts receivable	$200,000
Other assets	$50,000
Total balance sheet asset (book value)	$1,150,000
Patents	$1,000,000
Total assets	$2,150,000

The income statements for the previous five years show that the company's average annual earnings have been $450,000 for that period.

The business value was determined by using the years purchase method formula:

1. Average annual earnings in last five years	$450,000
2. Less assumed return on book value of $1,150,000 at 7%	−$80,500
3. Excess earnings (not attributable to balance sheet assets)	$369,500
4. Excess earnings multiplied by three years	× 3
5. Total excess earnings	$1,108,500
6. Add the book value	+$1,150,000
7. Total value	$2,258,500

Using that value in the formula for computing the periodic payments at Bill's age for his lifetime, he will receive an annual retirement income of $265,000.

■ SUMMARY

This chapter has examined the common methods used to value a business and has addressed the discounts that may apply to a minority interest or to one on which there are severe marketability limitations. It has stressed the imprecise nature of business valuation generally and the need for an evaluation of a range of factors, tempered by a substantial serving of common sense in valuing a business. The factors that suggest the use of one valuation method over another were also discussed.

Finally, the subject of incorporation of the valuation method into the buy-sell agreement was examined. Various examples of valuation provisions were seen that incorporate the different methods into the agreement.

■ CHAPTER 6 QUESTIONS FOR REVIEW

1. Which of the following valuation methods focuses entirely on the tangible business assets?

   A. Discounted cash flow

   B. Book value

   C. Straight capitalization

   D. Years purchase method

2. What would be the business value, using the straight capitalization method, of a business with average annual earnings of $100,000 and a capitalization factor of 20 percent?

   A. $20,000

   B. $100,000

   C. $500,000

   D. $1,000,000

3. In the straight capitalization method of business valuation, the capitalization rate used is intended to reflect which of the following?

   A. Likelihood that the business will outlive its owner

   B. Extent of the business' tangible assets

   C. Book value of the business assets

   D. Existing supplier credit terms

4. Which of the following assets would NOT generally be reflected on the business' balance sheet?

   A. Value of accounts receivable

   B. Value of fixtures

   C. Value of inventory

   D. Value of proprietary client list

5. Which of the following methods of business valuation does NOT reflect goodwill?

   A. Capitalization of earnings

   B. Straight capitalization

   C. Book value

   D. Years purchase method

····· Answer Key to Chapter Review Questions

Chapter 1

1. B
2. C
3. A
4. B
5. D

Chapter 2

1. C
2. D
3. B
4. A
5. C

Chapter 3

1. B
2. A
3. C
4. B
5. D

Chapter 4

1. B
2. C
3. A
4. D
5. B

Chapter 5

1. A
2. C
3. D
4. B
5. C

Chapter 6

1. B
2. C
3. A
4. D
5. C

Business Succession Planning
35-Question Multiple-Choice Examination

This exam is designed for those whose firms have selected this course for their firm element continuing education requirement. If the exam is to be graded and tracked by Dearborn, complete the answer sheet at the end of the book, using a black felt-tipped pen, and fax it to Dearborn at 312-836-1939. (To ensure accurate grading, each answer box must be completely filled in.)

If you don't know whether your firm has selected this course or whether Dearborn is to grade the exam, contact your compliance manager.

Note: This exam has not been approved for insurance continuing education and cannot be used for this purpose. If you need insurance continuing education credit for this course, a different exam is required. Contact Dearborn at 1-800-423-4723.

Business Succession Planning

1. Succession planning seeks to accomplish all of the following objectives EXCEPT

   A. ease the consequences on the business of the loss of the business owner
   B. minimize estate tax costs
   C. provide survivor income
   D. increase the cost basis of the business interest

2. What is the usual fate of a sole proprietorship upon the death of the business owner if the business owner's will contains no instructions to the contrary?

   A. Transfer of the business interest to other owners
   B. Liquidation of the business interest
   C. Sale of the business interest as a going concern
   D. Retention of the business interest in the family

3. What is the term applied to the liability of partners in a partnership?

   A. Absolute liability
   B. Pass-through liability
   C. Joint and several liability
   D. Limited liability

4. Liquidity is

   A. the ability to convert a business into cash quickly and with little or no loss in value
   B. another term for risk avoidance
   C. normally found in the estates of business owners
   D. normally provided through the business fixtures and buildings

5. Under normal circumstances, why would a personal representative be unwilling to continue to operate the decedent's business?

   A. A "hold harmless" provision in the decedent's will would not be effective to limit the personal representative's liability.
   B. The personal representative is required to share any losses with the decedent's estate.
   C. The personal representative may not have the skills needed to run the business properly.
   D. The personal representative is responsible for all losses that result.

6. A person whose death would have an adverse economic effect on the business caused by a loss of profits or credit standing is often considered a

   A. highly compensated employee
   B. key person
   C. party in interest
   D. fiduciary

7. Which of the following is generally considered to be the least attractive option for a business interest upon the death of the business owner?

   A. Selling the business to other owners
   B. Selling the business to employees
   C. Retaining the business in the family
   D. Liquidating the business

8. Which of the following would generally NOT be a factor favoring family retention of a business?

   A. Availability of successor management
   B. High profitability of the business
   C. Owning a minority interest in the business
   D. Tradition of family ownership

9. Who is responsible for wrapping up the affairs of the partnership upon the death of a partner?

   A. Deceased partner's executor
   B. Deceased partner's heirs
   C. Partner serving as a liquidating trustee
   D. Bankruptcy court

10. Under what circumstances would a surviving partner bear any loss suffered but not share in the profits of the partnership with the heirs?

    A. Whenever a partner dies
    B. When continuing to operate the partnership business without the consent of the former partner's heirs
    C. When the partner agreed to operate the business for a fee instead of profit participation
    D. Never; partners always share in both losses and profits

11. Under what circumstances would the surviving partners and the deceased partner's estate be assessed for partnership debts?

    A. Never; partnership debts are remitted upon the death of a partner
    B. When partnership debts exceed the liquidated value of partnership assets
    C. Only to the extent that partnership debts are owed to taxing authorities
    D. Never; partnership debts that exceed the partnership assets are payable only by surviving partners

12. Which one of the following organizations has a lifetime that is NOT legally affected by the death of an owner?

    A. Professional partnership
    B. Commercial corporation
    C. Commercial partnership
    D. Sole proprietorship

13. Which of the following would NOT generally be considered a benefit of establishing a value for a business in a buy-sell agreement?

    A. It eliminates the need to haggle over the value of the business upon the departure of an owner.
    B. It may set the value of the business for estate tax purposes.
    C. It enables the owners to more easily obtain the best price for the interest from outside buyers.
    D. It helps the parties to the agreement to plan for retirement and estate transfer.

14. What is the principal appeal of providing for funds to buy out a deceased co-stockholder's interest through life insurance?

    A. It is the most economical of the possible options.
    B. It increases the buyer's cost basis.
    C. It decreases the buyer's cost basis.
    D. It equalizes the cost among each of the stockholders.

15. Which of the following business entities is most likely to end at the death of a business owner?

    A. Corporation
    B. General partnership having a funded buy-sell agreement
    C. Sole proprietorship
    D. Limited partnership on the death of a limited partner

16. What is frequently a result of the need for a business owner's estate to pay estate taxes within nine months of the business owner's death?

    A. Liquidation of the business interest
    B. Sale of the business interest to other owners
    C. Retention of the business interest by the deceased business owner's family
    D. Sale of the business interest to outsiders

17. What is the definition of goodwill?

    A. Value of intangible assets
    B. Total of the depreciation taken on the company's balance sheet
    C. Difference between the value of the firm as a going concern and its asset value
    D. Gotal value of existing business contracts

18. Which of the following would NOT generally be a consequence of a forced liquidation sale?

    A. Compromise of accounts receivable
    B. Loss of goodwill
    C. Sale of the business as a going concern
    D. Sale of inventory, plant and fixtures at fire-sale prices

19. Which of the following factors would NOT be one favoring liquidation?

    A. Uninterested heirs
    B. Unavailable successor manager
    C. High risk business
    D. Goodwill is readily transferable

20. In which of the following situations would the lack of a license generally prohibit a potential buyer of a business interest from purchasing it?

    A. In a commercial partnership owning a new car dealership
    B. In a professional corporation providing health care
    C. In a sole proprietorship owning a restaurant
    D. In a commercial corporation selling consulting services

21. Which of the following testamentary provisions would NOT be one designed to minimize the erosion of business value on liquidation?

    A. Power to sell the business
    B. Power to retain the business
    C. Hold harmless provision
    D. Power to loan business funds

22. Which of the following is an essential purpose of planning for business liquidation?

    A. To increase the heirs' cost basis
    B. To minimize business value erosion
    C. To find a successor owner
    D. To avoid estate taxes

23. Which of the following would NOT normally be considered an estate settlement cost?

    A. Cost to provide income to survivors
    B. Federal estate taxes
    C. State death taxes
    D. Probate costs

24. What is the major role of life insurance in the planned liquidation of a business interest?

    A. Paying estate settlement costs
    B. Providing interim working capital
    C. Funding a buy-sell agreement
    D. Replacing the value of the business lost through liquidation

25. Which of the following would NOT normally be an advantage to the surviving family of life insurance on the business owner's life in the case of business liquidation?

    A. Funding a buy-sell agreement
    B. Providing income to the family
    C. Allowing the family to receive the value that the business has as an ongoing business
    D. Insurance proceeds may avoid probate costs and claims of creditors

26. What provision is ordinarily made to enable the executor to provide estate liquidity in the case of a retained business interest?

    A. The executor is given the power to borrow against the estate's assets.
    B. The executor is given the power to invade the corpus of any trusts.
    C. The executor is given the power to use corporate assets.
    D. The executor is empowered to assess the heirs.

27. Which of the following would be a concern of an intended gifting strategy for transfer of the business interest to family members upon the business owner's disability?

   A. Possible income taxes
   B. Family attribution rules
   C. Possible gift taxes
   D. Possible estate taxes

28. In addition to providing the funding for a disability buyout, what additional function can the disability insurance policy perform?

   A. Establish the criteria for determining the business owner's disability
   B. Provide funds to pay estate taxes
   C. Increase the business owner's cost basis for the business interest
   D. Cause the transaction to avoid income taxes

29. Under what circumstances would the use of a private annuity to purchase a family business interest result in the payment of gift taxes?

   A. Gift taxes are never required in the case of a private annuity.
   B. When the private annuity is for less than full and adequate consideration.
   C. Gift taxes are due only to the extent of the difference between the value of the business interest and the sum of private annuity payments actually made.
   D. In every case, because as a gift of a future interest it would not qualify for the gift tax exclusion.

30. The seller of a business interest funded by a private annuity cannot spread the gain over more than one year when the

   A. seller's cost basis is less than 50 percent of the value of the business interest
   B. sale is made to a family member
   C. promise to make annuity payments is secured
   D. total of the private annuity payments is less than the value of the business interest

31. In which of the following can the seller of a business interest expect to receive payments for life?

   A. Self-canceling installment note
   B. Private annuity
   C. Regular installment note
   D. Lump-sum payment

32. Under which of the following is a risk premium normally required to account for the possibility that the obligation to continue payments will be extinguished upon the payee's death?

   A. Private annuity
   B. SCIN
   C. Regular installment note
   D. Commercial paper

33. When a firm takes depreciation on its book value, the book value

   A. is increased
   B. is unaffected
   C. is decreased
   D. more accurately reflects fair market value

34. Which of the following assets would NOT generally be included in a company's book value?

   A. Patents
   B. Accounts receivable
   C. Land
   D. Buildings

35. Under which of the following valuation methods is there likely to be the least amount of misunderstanding concerning the value of the business?

   A. Discounted cash flow
   B. Straight capitalization
   C. Agreed value
   D. Years purchase method